AMERICAN HERITAGE
ILLUSTRATED HISTORY
OF THE UNITED STATES

A view of the State House in Philadelphia in 1799.

FRONT COVER: *Detail of a painting of the English expedition under General Braddock being ambushed by the French and Indians.*
STATE HISTORICAL SOCIETY OF WISCONSIN

FRONT ENDSHEET: *New France's Governor Frontenac orders an Indian tortured.*
ONONDAGA HISTORICAL ASSOCIATION

CONTENTS PAGE: *A detail of a Dutch map depicts the 1650 image of America.*
NEW YORK PUBLIC LIBRARY; STOKES COLLECTION

BACK ENDSHEET: *The English assault at Freshwater Cove, near Louisburg.*
MABEL BRADY GARVAN COLLECTION, YALE UNIVERSITY ART GALLERY

BACK COVER: *Detail of engraving of the State House in Philadelphia in 1799 (top left); Slaves dancing in watercolor depiction—possibly of a wedding—in the late eighteenth century (top right); detail of painting (bottom) of Pilgrims walking to church.*
ABBY ALDRICH ROCKEFELLER FOLK ART COLLECTION, WILLIAMSBURG, VIRGINIA; NEW YORK PUBLIC LIBRARY; NEW YORK HISTORICAL SOCIETY

AMERICAN HERITAGE
ILLUSTRATED HISTORY
OF THE UNITED STATES

VOLUME 2

COLONIAL AMERICA

LIBRARY EDITION
with Index in Volume 19

SILVER BURDETT PRESS, INC.

1989

Library of Congress Catalog Card Number: 89-50419
ISBN 0-382-09859-5 (Vol. 2)
ISBN 0-382-09878-1 (Set)

This 1989 revised edition is published and distributed by Silver Burdett Press, Inc., Prentice Hall Building, Englewood Cliffs, NJ 07632 by arrangement with American Heritage, a division of Forbes, Inc.

Manufactured in the United States of America

AMERICAN HERITAGE
ILLUSTRATED HISTORY
OF THE UNITED STATES

VOLUME 2

COLONIAL AMERICA

BY ROBERT G. ATHEARN

Created in Association with the
Editors of AMERICAN HERITAGE

and for the updated edition
MEDIA PROJECTS INCORPORATED

CHOICE PUBLISHING, INC.
New York

Library of Congress Catalog Card Number: 87-73399
ISBN 0-945260-02-4
ISBN 0-945260-00-8

This 1988 edition is published and distributed by Choice Publishing, Inc., 53 Watermill Lane, Great Neck, NY 11021
by arrangement with American Heritage, a division of Forbes, Inc.

Manufactured in the United States of America
10 9 8 7 6 5 4 3

CONTENTS OF THE COMPLETE SERIES

Editor's Note to the Revised Edition
Introduction by ALLAN NEVINS
Main text by ROBERT G. ATHEARN

EACH VOLUME CONTAINS AN ENCYCLOPEDIC SECTION; MASTER INDEX IN VOLUME 18

CONTENTS OF VOLUME 2

CHAPTER 4

THE COLONIES GROW

From the seedlings that were Plymouth and Jamestown, English settlements spread out all along the Atlantic seacoast. While the Cape Cod region was somewhat less attractive than the more verdant land of Virginia, it was here that the first real population growth occurred. Hardly had the Pilgrims set up their village at Plymouth before their own promoter, Thomas Weston, sent out a group of rowdy individuals to settle nearby and establish a fishing post. Irresponsible, ignorant of the demands of a New England winter, the latest arrivals neglected to plant crops or make other necessary preparations. Their settlement was a failure.

Not far away another attempt floundered and finally came under the control of Thomas Morton, who rocked conservative New England to its foundations by turning his colony into the gayest settlement in America. Calling his place Merry Mount, he put up an enormous Maypole around which his men danced, drank, and

John Eliot was preacher to the Indians and translator of the Bible into their language. He was 55 when painted in 1659.

frolicked with the Indians and their women. As the natives approved, and brought their beaver skins to Merry Mount instead of Plymouth, the Pilgrims watched the continuous party with righteous indignation.

By 1628, there were several communities planted along the shores of Massachusetts Bay. A fishing post started in 1623 at Cape Ann, on the north rim, was unsuccessful, but those who refused to go home moved southward to found the town of Salem. The residents sent word to England that their little community would be a haven for those dissatisfied with the religious situation at home. They were answered by a Reverend John White of Dorchester, an Anglican minister who, although unhappy with the official church, did not want to separate in the manner of Pilgrims. He and his followers became known as Puritans, since they hoped merely to purify the church, not destroy it. By appealing to some London businessmen, who saw economic opportunity in America, White sparked the formation of the New England Company. It was given a charter in 1628, and at once sent out John Endecott as director.

One of his first official acts in America was to send Miles Standish across Massachusetts Bay to Merry Mount to chop down poor Morton's Maypole. Colonizing was supposed to be a serious business!

In 1629, the New England Company was rechartered under the name of the Massachusetts Bay Company. Like the Mayflower Compact, the new charter was to be significant in American history. Because of the insistence of Puritan squire John Winthrop, who wanted to sponsor a small emigration, there would be no governing council in England. The control of the colony would be in America. That condition satisfied, Winthrop was elected governor and organization proceeded. By the next spring the company was transferred to America. During that year 840 immigrants arrived in Massachusetts; it was the largest group yet to leave

home. Significantly, the arrivals represented not only workers but some men of means who had qualities of leadership. Understandably, 1630 is called the year of the great migration —caused by discontent with Charles I, who ignored Parliament and was arbitrary in both political and religious matters. The Massachusetts Bay Colony was not without food shortages and personal suffering, but after the first few years, growth was rapid. By 1643, the population stood somewhere between 14,000 and 16,000, which was perhaps more than the entire population of England's other American colonies.

Colonies breed colonies

At a rather tender age the Massachusetts Bay Colony gave birth to a whole litter of small colonies. Within three or four years after Winthrop's arrival, outposts from both the Pil-

The four ships John Winthrop brought to New England (left) are anchored in Boston harbor, where his group settled after first landing at Salem, the colony governed by the Puritan John Endecott (above).

grims' settlement and those along the bay were established in the fertile Connecticut Valley, and America's great westward movement was launched.

Within a few years, after having allied to ward off the Pequot Indians, several towns along the valley joined to frame an agreement that called for self-government. Removed not only from England but the coastal settlements as well, these people found it necessary to take things into their own hands. The Fundamental Orders of Connecticut, while not particularly liberal, provided some political safeguards that marked a gain in the quest for a measure of local control.

New Hampshire and Maine were also offspring of Massachusetts. Lack of interest in them by their sponsors, coupled with the fact that the residents (who had come largely from Massachusetts) looked more and more to the older colony for guidance, spelled their failure as independent enterprises. In 1644, after a few struggling years, New Hampshire was taken over by the Bay Colony; a similar absorption of Maine took place 14 years later. Not until 1679 would New Hampshire again become a separate colony, and Maine would remain a part of Massachusetts until 1820, when it became a state in the Union.

More independent were the little settlements in Rhode Island. The leaders there were two dissidents named Roger Williams and Anne Hutchinson. Williams, one of the most original thinkers in America of his time, believed the church in Massachusetts was not separate enough from the Anglican church and that it meddled too much in politics. So loud was his complaint about this and such requirements as taxation to support religion and compulsory attend-

97

ance that in 1635 he was banished from Massachusetts. He promptly established his followers at Providence, Rhode Island. He was joined by Mrs. Hutchinson, who, with her exiles, settled at a place later known as Portsmouth. Williams next went to London and got a charter for his colony, despite the bitter opposition of the Massachusetts Bay powers. Thus legitimatized, Rhode Island went forward in its development, and by insisting upon complete separation of church and state, carved another support for American democracy.

The rapid spread of the Connecticut frontier produced problems. Typically, the whites refused to recognize Indian claims, insisting that cultiva-tion proved ownership, and before long there was violence. The settlers appealed to Boston for help, but the situation was so pressing that they were obliged to raise a force for their own defense. Volunteers, led by experienced Indian fighters, attacked the natives, and before the battle was over, 500 Pequots were burned alive or killed as they tried to flee. The rest were enslaved or sold in the West Indies. For the next 250 years, in succeeding Western settlements, the story would be the same.

Out of the bloody affair there arose the Confederation of New England —colonial settlements joined for mutual protection. Organized in 1643, the Confederation was a "firm and

Roger Williams, banished from Massachusetts in 1635 for his liberal views, is shown landing in Rhode Island in an 1858 painting by Alonzo Chappel.

perpetual league of friendship" and stands as the first attempt at a confederacy of colonies in North America. Aside from its defense duties, the league aimed to provide its members with such services as the return of runaway servants, escaped prisoners, and other law violators. Under some circumstances it even proposed to make treaties with foreign powers. Perhaps its founders were too optimistic; within 20 years the Confederation began to disintegrate. Aside from the bickering that took place, and the attempted dominance of Massachusetts, England itself frowned upon the league's efforts to engage in diplomatic relations with the French and Dutch over their colonies, which flanked New England. The conquest of New Netherland by the English in 1664 eased one of the major pressures that originally had inspired the union. Despite its transitory nature, however, the Confederation taught a lesson in the virtues of cooperation that would be remembered at a later and more critical time.

The lords go west

Not all the English colonies in America were managed by joint enterprise. Maryland, for example, owes its origin to George Calvert, the first Lord Baltimore, who in 1632 was granted a charter by the king. Calvert's older son Cecilius took over the grant upon his father's death and became the proprietor of a 10,000,000-acre feudal estate in the wilds of North America. All he owed the king were two Indian arrows a year and one-fifth of the gold and silver found upon the land. This was merely a recognition of the king as feudal superior, and as few or no precious metals were found, young Calvert could not complain about high taxes.

Cecilius Calvert, who now became Lord Baltimore, and his young brother Leonard managed their colony well. Although they were Catholics, they allowed extensive liberties to Protestants who wanted to settle. As businessmen, they were more interested in making a profit than in quarreling over religious beliefs. Thanks to such sound judgment, Maryland prospered from the beginning, and while there were no magnificent returns, there was also no starvation period. To show they were sincere in their desire for religious toleration, the Calverts caused to be passed in 1649 an Act Concerning Religion. The Puritan-controlled assembly did not produce an act as liberal as Lord Baltimore wished, but it provided an encouraging basis for future legislation.

Politically the colony followed a course of increasing liberality. For the first few years Leonard Calvert governed it personally, but in 1637, Cecilius, who had never come to Maryland, directed Leonard to call together the local council. At first the council had no power, but gradually it assumed some, and by 1642 it held that, like the English Parliament, it had the right to convene when it saw fit. By 1650, it had been divided into two houses, with a majority in both required for the passage of laws.

Socially there was less democracy. In the early period there were about 60 manors, each from 1,000 to 3,000 acres, managed by nobles and worked by commoners. The gap between these classes was wide. In a country with so much free land to the west, such a system could not prosper and eventually competition took its toll on privilege as the estates broke up. Out of the inadequacies of a feudal system on the frontier, there developed in Maryland not only broad social equality but a local self-government that made a great contribution to political self-sufficiency in America. The colonists here, as in New England, gained experience that served them well later on.

As Maryland became firmly established, there were multiplying pressures in England that were to result in further migration. By 1640, the breach between Parliament and Charles I had become too great to heal. The legislators assembled and refused to be dispersed for nine years, becoming known as the Long Parliament. By 1642, actual warfare broke out and the Puritan Revolution was in full swing. After resisting for four years the king surrendered and, in 1649, was executed. Oliver Cromwell now dominated the scene until he died. In 1660, Charles II was invited to the throne; the English were willing to try a monarch again. With his accession, colonial growth, which had been slowed in

previous years, speeded up. During the next quarter century, three more of the 13 colonies were established—Pennsylvania and the two Carolinas—and New Netherland, taken from the Dutch, became the English colonies of New Jersey and New York.

The Carolinas—strange sisters

In the spring of 1663, Charles II indicated that a new era in colonization was under way when he granted eight of his courtiers a generous slice of the Atlantic seaboard called Carolina. It was the greatest single unoccupied piece of land between Virginia and Spanish Florida, lying between the 36th and the 31st parallels. While the promoters put profit first, the move meant more than economic gain; it was a bold thrust at Spain. When in 1665 the charter was expanded to the 29th parallel, boldly taking in Spanish St. Augustine, Charles II indicated that England was again on the march in America. In this great real estate venture the proprietors planned to sell off portions of land.

Socially and politically, the founders hoped to reproduce English society in America with a structure comprised of nobles at the top and tenants and other dependents below. For a type of government favorable to their notions, they engaged the famous John Locke to prepare the Fundamental Constitutions of Carolina. It projected a strictly aristocratic way of life in a sparsely settled wilderness—a caste system with bluebloods in

In March, 1634, Maryland was settled by a group of 200 that included two Jesuits and many Roman Catholics from England. Painted by Emanuel Leutze.

complete control. For 20 years the proprietors forced their grand political document against the abrasive of frontier conditions, until it became a useless piece of parchment. Commoners who left England partially to avoid such conditions would have none of it. Southern Carolina was the scene of the more serious colonizing effort. In 1670, after several unsuccessful attempts farther north, a settlement called Charles Town was established. It would be relocated in 1680, on the present site of Charleston. The northern part of Carolina was not developed; it just grew. Its people were mainly small farmers of the independent frontier type, and they looked with suspicion upon the more feudal society south of them. It is not surprising that in 1691 Carolina was divided. The decision was a wise one, for as the 17th century progressed, South Carolina developed into a plantation, rice-raising type of colony, politically conservative and socially stratified. Its sister colony meanwhile expanded along quite different lines. Comprised largely of poor men, who strongly objected to any taxation, North Carolina was a land of smuggling, general lawbreaking, and extreme individualism. Both sections, however, had one important thing in common: They were peopled more by overflow from other American colonies than emigration from England, and provide an excellent example of that method of expansion in colonial America.

Other bits of patronage

When Charles II came to the throne after 12 years in exile and much in debt, he not only repaid loyal followers who had spent their own fortunes in his behalf by giving them huge grants of land in America. He also gave his brother, the Duke of York, the rich colony of New Netherland, recently wrested from the Dutch, stretching between the Connecticut and Delaware Rivers. It included a bit of real estate of great potential value known as Long Island. As in the case of the other proprietary colonies, the duke was to be the sole ruler, merely acknowledging feudal loyalty to the monarch by the annual payment of 40 beaver skins. There was no legislative body, and the only restraint upon York was the requirement that his laws conform fairly well with those at home. Obviously, he had a good deal of leeway.

From the beginning, New York, renamed by its new proprietor, was ruled by an iron hand. The duke, who was later to rule England itself as the unpopular James II, had ample opportunity to school himself in the fine points of being a king. The colony was recaptured by the Dutch in 1673, only to be returned one year later

This map titled A Description of the Towne of Mannados *shows Dutch New Amsterdam in 1661. As the English-owned colony of New York, it was governed by Sir Edmund Andros (above), 1674–81.*

as England triumphed over Holland. In the following years arbitrary government was resumed under the strict guidance of Sir Edmund Andros. In 1683, after years of complaint from the people, representative government came into being with the calling of the assembly. But due to disturbing delays, New Yorkers would have to wait almost another decade before they had any voice in their own affairs. Yet, despite the restrictiveness of its government, the colony developed well economically. Agriculture and trade increased, and an active commerce in furs with the Indians laid down a prosperous foundation.

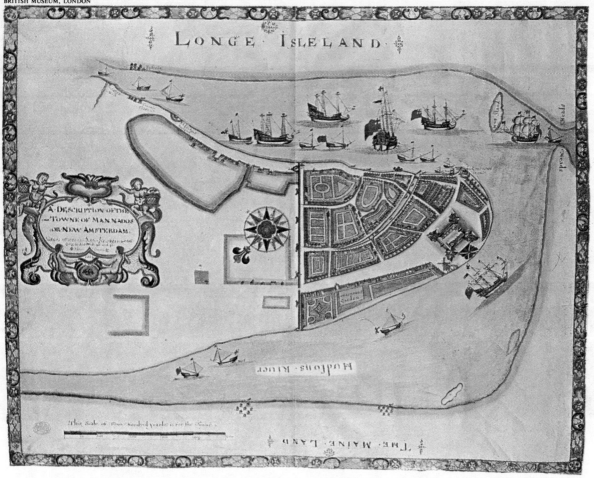

New Jersey resulted from the establishment of New York. Not long after the Duke of York received his charter, he signed over the land lying between the Hudson and Delaware Rivers to Lord John Berkeley and Sir George Carteret, who had helped greatly in restoring the Stuarts to the throne. The new proprietors, who were members of the original group that founded Carolina, named their new possession New Jersey in honor of one of them who had served as governor of the Island of Jersey. They were interested in their latest real estate venture primarily for profit. After a welter of sales and a resulting confusion of title claims, the proprietors finally surrendered their political powers to the crown in 1702. In the meantime, a curious assortment of Quakers, Catholics, and Presbyterians were in control of the little patch of land.

The Quakers buy in

Among the Quakers interested in New Jersey was a young man named William Penn. He had contributed to its new constitution of 1677, called the most liberal of its time, and had otherwise participated in the colonial experiment. When Penn's father died, Charles II owed him some 16,000

After William Penn's arrival in America in 1682, he established friendly relations with the Indians, as Benjamin West portrayed in this 1771 painting.

pounds, and in keeping with his policy of paying off in land, he now offered young William a sizable tract in America. Already interested in colonizing, Penn accepted and received his grant in 1681. The land, to which would soon be added three counties of Delaware (later partially separated from Pennsylvania in 1704), comprised an area almost as large as England itself. For this Penn owed the king nothing more than the customary beaver skins annually and one-fifth of any gold and silver he might discover. Nevertheless, he was more responsible to the king than either the Duke of York or Lord Baltimore.

A small council—elected by taxpayers from leading landowners—initiated bills, and a large elected assembly passed on them. But the governor had wide powers of appointment. The colony was in many respects a feudal domain, yet its proprietor was popular. One reason was the liberal government set up by the constitution. It provided for its own amendments, as does our own. Impeachment of officials offered a check on arbitrary power. Penn even suggested that laws inconsistent with the constitution were void, although it would be over 100 years before the courts would rule on unconstitutionality. Thus many motions advanced by the Quakers are a part of our law and tradition today.

The colonists who came to Pennsylvania suffered fewer physical hardships than earlier arrivals. Penn himself arrived in the fall of 1682, and within a year about 3,000 immigrants had landed and Philadelphia had 80 houses. Compared to other colonies, the Quaker settlement developed rapidly. There was plenty of food, little sickness, and no danger from the Indians. In 1684, the founder was obliged to return to England to settle a land dispute with Lord Baltimore. He did not return to America until 1699.

The same year Penn made his settlement, French explorers covered thousands of tortuous miles to lay claim to the Mississippi Valley. That spring Robert Cavelier de La Salle planted his nation's standard at the river's mouth and, calling the land Louisiana, claimed the American West. These events, in a single year, point up the differences in colonizing methods. As the two claims edged toward each other, empires would collide.

Georgia—buffer against Spain

By the end of the 17th century, the English had firmly established an unbroken line of colonies from New England southward to the Carolinas. As the proprietors of the latter had not heavily sprinkled their lands with settlers, and because Spain edged northward from Florida rather un-

certainly, the English decided to wedge in another colony. In 1732, George II granted a charter to a group of trustees headed by James Oglethorpe providing for a settlement to be named Georgia.

Political and religious developments in England dictated a change in methods of colonizing, and Oglethorpe's charter therefore differed from all others. In 1688, the English middle classes triumphed in the revolution of that year and promptly forced the passage of a toleration act granting freedom of public worship to dissenters. This meant that political and religious motives for colonization, once quite strong, were now minimized. Experience dictated still another modification: Time had shown that corporate colonies did not make a substantial profit for their sponsors. Also to the detriment of the mother country was the practice of granting wide political powers to these incorporators as a means of making their projects attractive to emigrants. All that resulted was a weakening of the hold upon such colonies.

Neither individual money-making, religious freedom, nor political independence were the prime movers; the forces at work behind this venture lay with the government itself. Oglethorpe was primarily a humanitarian, and his desire to empty the English jails of debtors coincided with the government's wish to plant a buffer colony snug against Spanish Florida. The charter provided that the trustees

James Oglethorpe's humanitarian idea brought men from the debtors' prisons to lands in Georgia.

should get no personal gain from the venture and must be under the strict control of the crown, and that Georgia would become a royal province within 21 years. Money for the project came from two sources—funds solicited from private philanthropic organizations and grants directly from Parliament. So the government of Georgia was unlike its predecessors; it was paternalistic in nature and controlled from above. As in the case of the others, however, frontier pressure finally led in 1751 to the granting of assembly privileges. It was no real step toward democracy, for a council and governor, both appointed, held the reins of power and the colony was run by remote control.

How England kept her hold

From Jamestown to Georgia, for 125 years, the English carved out colony after colony along the Atlantic seaboard. These were years of experimentation, of radically changing conditions at home, and of shifting international power. The result was three principal types of ventures—royal, proprietary, and chartered. With a variety of people settling for diverse reasons, it might seem that the result would be a hodgepodge. But regardless of the patchwork appearance, there were strong threads running through the organizations, with the ends securely held at home.

Whatever its type, each colony had a governor, and while he was chief executive of his own domain, he was always the agent of the crown. Even in the two charter colonies, where the governor was elected, he was answerable to higher authority. In the proprietary colonies, where he received his appointment from the proprietor, his selection was first passed upon in England. This official stood between local legislatures, often liberal in attitude, and the mother country, whose interests were at stake. Not only did he represent the king directly in political matters; he was commander-in-chief of the local militia and acted in a diplomatic capacity by carrying on

Oglethorpe's promise of a new beginning in a new world filled Europe's down-trodden with hope. Among those who responded were persecuted Lutherans from Salzburg, shown in this 1732 engraving as they depart for Georgia.

relations with neighboring colonies. Furthermore, he could appoint vice-admiralty court judges, ordinary judges, justices of the peace, and sheriffs. All in all, his influence and powers were widespread and effective. Naturally, he was often the subject of bitter criticism from the independent-minded colonials who came to expect a no to their every request. Criticized in America, and often reprimanded by the home government, the governor's job was a lonely one. Inevitably perhaps, Americans later created a similar position for their own "colonies," and the same complaints echoed again from the Western territories in the 19th century.

Colonial connection with England was further extended in local legislatures. As a rule, it was the governor who called these bodies into session, although in some cases the legislature had the right to meet at least every three years despite the executive's wishes. However, no legislature could make a law effective without the governor's signature; in effect, he held an absolute veto. Should he not be inclined to exercise so direct a power, he could simply suspend a proposed law while he asked advice from the home government. The upper legislative house, called the council, was usually appointed, and almost without exception its members came from the more influential colonists of the upper classes. They were conservative in their thinking and more likely to have the monarch's interests at heart. The lower house, known as the assembly, was elected by colonial property owners and was therefore often similarly conservative. For example, in Pennsylvania one had to own 50 acres to be a qualified voter. While the lower house held the purse strings, as it does in our national government, and could wield great power, both the upper house and the governor had adequate means of checking any radical tendencies. One nuisance value the assembly often had was the right to earmark funds, which controlled the governor in his spending. Exercising the right did little to improve his disposition.

Despite the fact that the typical colonist wasn't treated as a first-class citizen, he managed—like the middle class in England—to nibble away at precedent and gradually gain more privileges. In the assembly his friends chipped away at the governor's position, worrying him about appropriating his pay, insisting that they alone had the authority to appoint the colonial treasurer, demanding the right to authorize military expeditions, and finally claiming they could send agents to represent them in London. While the assemblies did not always get their way, the seesaw battle edged in their direction. They were moving, slowly but certainly, toward a parliamentary form of government, and from their tribulations came experience that later served them well when the final break came with England. Gradually the friction of shifting conditions wore away at the string that held the colonial pearls together.

Spare the rod . . .

During the busy years of the 18th century, Mother England was like the old woman who lived in a shoe. She had so many children she didn't know what to do. But instead of spanking them soundly and putting them to bed, she fumbled and temporized. Members of the rapidly growing Empire family assumed that the customary "rights of Englishmen" were unaltered by distance from home. For decades, governing officials at London failed to challenge the assumption.

By the time they awakened to the fact that American colonists had accustomed themselves to a course of independent action in their day-to-day dealings, matters had gone too far to be corrected even by force. Men in America, long in the habit of shifting for themselves despite the attempts of colonial governors to check them, would not listen to disciplinary talk from faraway London. They had tasted the fruits of parental neglect, and they found the sensation to their liking.

THE FRENCH
AND INDIAN WARS

It was inevitable that England and France should clash in the New World. They had been in conflict for generations in Europe, and they had not improved their relations in North America, where their empires lay side by side. The struggle lasted for 70 years. It began in 1690 with the massacre by French and Indian raiders of English settlers at Schenectady, New York, and ended with the capture by the English of Quebec in 1759 and Montreal in 1760. Four colonial wars were fought within the 70-year span—King William's War, Queen Anne's War, King George's War, and the French and Indian War. This last and most important conflict gave its name to the whole series of wars. It began in 1754, and proved to be the beginning of the end of French power in North America. For despite their close alliances with the Indians, the French were never able to overcome the disadvantage of their small population in Canada and their lack of organized colonies. The English colonials were established settlers—family men willing to die defending their homes and farms.

THE REDCOATS

The English soldier at the left is a member of the 44th Foot, one of the regiments sent to America in 1755 to break French control of the Ohio Valley. They were commanded by General Braddock.

Sir Joshua Reynolds' young officer (right) is Captain Robert Orme, Braddock's favorite aide on the march into the Ohio country. He knew no more about wilderness warfare than his general did.

Braddock's men march through the wilderness in orderly European columns, to the sound of fife and drums. Their target is Fort Duquesne, the French base located on the site of present-day Pittsburgh.

The English expedition is ambushed by the French and Indians as they approach Fort

Duquesne. General Braddock would still not let his troops take cover in the Indian style.

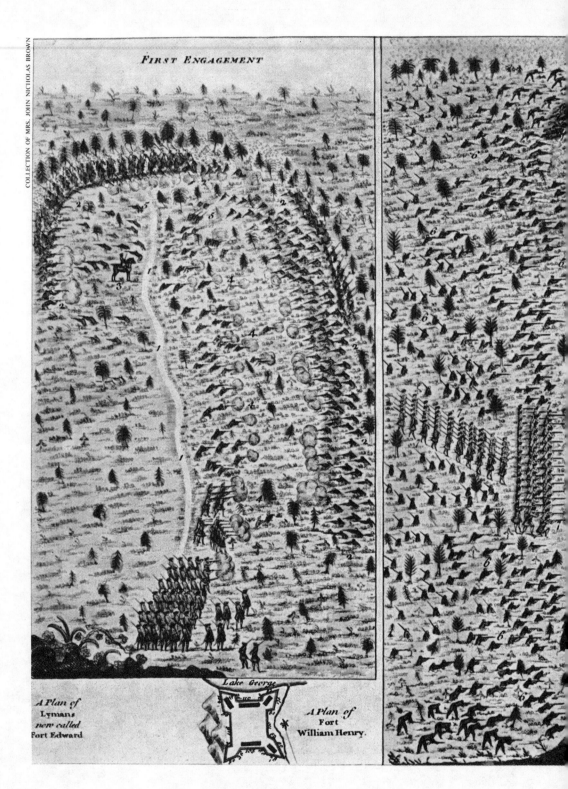

FIRST ENGAGEMENT

*A Plan of
Lymans
now called
Fort Edward*

Lake George

*A Plan of
Fort
William Henry.*

THE FRENCH AND INDIAN WARS

THE BATTLE AT LAKE GEORGE

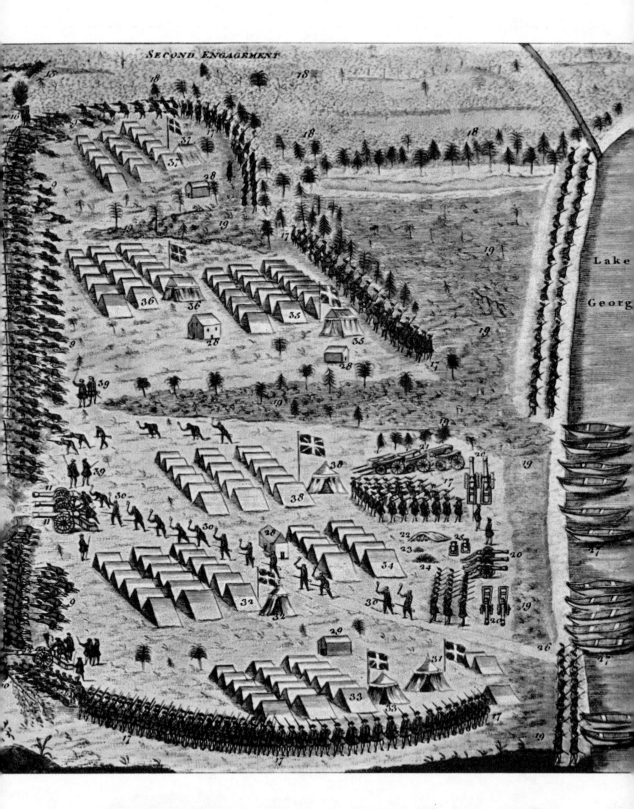

The French suffered a major defeat when they met the English on the shores of Lake George in 1755. In this print by an eyewitness, the English, in blue uniforms (left), were first surprised by a French ambush; later, in red uniforms (right), they triumphed.

LAKE CHAMPLAIN

LIBRARY OF CONGRESS

The French lost control of Lake Champlain in 1759, and in doing so, they opened to the English the southern route to Canada. English troops, led by Major General Jeffrey Amherst (opposite), took the important French forts controlling the lake—Crown Point (above) and Ticonderoga (below). Amherst was commander of the English forces in America. His portrait is by Reynolds.

NEW-YORK HISTORICAL SOCIETY

THE SIEGE OF QUEBEC

On the morning of September 13, 1759, the struggle for Quebec, capital of France's North American empire, began. The English army, commanded by Major General James Wolfe, had already engaged the French on the Plains of Abraham above the city, as British reinforcements were being brought ashore.

Louis Joseph, Marquis de Montcalm, led the French defense of Quebec. He was mortally wounded as the French began to lose their desperate battle to the English.

OVERLEAF: James Wolfe (center), surrounded by his officers as he lay dying on the Plains of Abraham, had lived long enough to see his English troops winning their battle with the French. Quebec, and with it all of French Canada, would soon fall. Wolfe is reported to have said, after he was shot, "Now God be praised. Since I have conquered, I will die in peace."

NATIONAL GALLERY OF CANADA, OTTAWA

PUBLIC ARCHIVES OF CANADA

TRINITY CHURCH, SAINT JOHN, NEW BRUNSWICK

CHAPTER 5

STRUGGLE FOR POWER

The westward expansion of colonial America developed a sectional
problem that was first to plague England and later influence the growth of
the United States. As settlers moved
inland from the coastal area and ascended the lower slopes of the Appalachians, they were separated from
their neighbors to the east by water-
falls that prevented a navigable connection. If one were to draw a north-
south line touching these falls, there
would emerge what is called the fall
line. As imaginary as the equator, it
nevertheless divided the early settlers
into the tidewater and piedmont residents. (The latter term refers to an up-
country plateau lying between the fall
line and the crest of the mountains.)

Piedmonters found that while com-
munication with the coastal people
was now more difficult, a north-south
movement was relatively easy, and the
continual flow of population up and
down molded a section that could
call itself Western. Corralled by geog-
raphy, the newcomers banded together

*The French coat of arms (top) once ap-
peared on the gates of Quebec, and the British arms (bottom) hung in the city of Boston.*

in common cause, and conscious of
their remoteness and newness, hooted
in derision at those who had been
lucky enough to pre-empt seaboard
sites. Often without regard to fact,
they looked upon the tidewater people
as "aristocrats" who were bent upon
monopolizing power and privilege for
themselves. It was the usual case of
the majority clinging to what it had
gained and the minority striving for
what it wanted.

There was just enough truth in the
frontiersmen's charges to make their
cause sound plausible, particularly in
the West. Many a small Western landowner was in debt to tidewater specu-
lators for land he had bought. In addition to being hounded for payment,
he was obliged to sell what few products he raised for profit to the specu-
lators at whatever price was offered.
The usual animosity of a debtor class
to a creditor class resulted, and it is
not surprising that those along the
frontier convinced themselves that the
economic game was rigged in favor
of the dealers.

It was in this first West that an
American population was born. While
it was comprised of a number of na-

123

tionalities, English, German, and Scotch-Irish contributed the predominant strains. They were generally small farmers in a land almost wholly agricultural. There were no domains with their semi-feudal lords of the very early colonial type. The piedmonters lived in an isolation that not only demanded self-preservation but demanded it so strongly that ethnic lines were obliterated in the face of common defense. Outside forces like the elements and the Indians pressed this frontier into a compact ideological community.

Other straws that bound the clay of Western society were the dissatisfactions of its members with the Europe they had left. If they were not joined in a common dislike of the old country, they at least shared a lack of interest in it. The sentiment was not only to affect the course of English colonial development but to have deep influences on the later history of American diplomacy.

Western expansion had a long-range effect upon American development, and during the 18th and 19th centuries it showed up clearly on the national scene. Westerners on succeeding frontiers continued to be an independent, vocal lot, negotiating often with other foreign powers (especially Spain) in order to wring advantages first from England and later from the United States. They experimented freely in government, social organization, and even communal living, to the unfailing distaste of the more conservative East. By the end of the 19th century, American historians were talking about the significance of the West upon national growth, and universities were experimenting with courses dealing with the westward movement.

English pressure mounts

Until the middle of the 18th century, England made no effort to control the expansion of her American colonies. The more people of any nationality who buttressed her holdings, the stronger her relative position became. Spain had got off to a fast start in colonizing and had laid claim to

124

On April 9, 1682, La Salle reached the mouth of the Mississippi. Here he claimed the river and the lands it drained for Louis XIV of France, naming the huge territory Louisiana in the king's honor.

most of the Western Hemisphere. By 1700, the day of the conquistadors was about over and the first flush of conquest had abated. Most of the quick money had been milked from Spanish America, and in the days ahead a more solid economic basis would have to be found to make Spain's claims hold up. For over 200 years, since the days of Columbus, she had squandered her American gold, quarreling with other Continental powers.

The 18th century was to see the Spanish on the defensive and the English ever ready to contribute to their downfall. No fewer than eight times in a little over 100 years the two nations went to war. As Spain poured out her treasure, trying to keep back the intruders, England merely grew in stature and attained for herself the reputation of being mistress of the seas. In 1763, in the Treaty of Paris, England got East and West Florida. By 1790, Spain was in such a weakened condition that her day as a great colonizer was nearly over.

As English colonists filtered through the Appalachian passes, pressing their claims against Spain's, another nation worried about such steady expansion. The Canadian French had swept around the northern end of England's colonial frontier and plunged deep into the continent along the Great Lakes and down the Mississippi Valley. Their American empire depended upon furs and thus was loosely organized with vast stretches of land between settlements. With the exception of the Iroquois, with whom they fought constantly, the French were friendly with the Indians. The natives generally could be counted upon as their allies.

This was important, for, like the Spanish, the French had been unable to populate heavily the lands they claimed. They realized their weakness as England's strong young offspring relentlessly pressed forward. To be prepared for the inevitable collision, the French tried a policy of containment by building a ring of forts around the oncoming English. From Fort Niagara in the north to Fort Toulouse on the Alabama River, they blocked out a line of defense. Crown Point, on Lake Champlain, was fortified to check any English overflow out of the valleys of the Connecticut or Hudson Rivers. But despite all precautions, the hold of the French was too weak to withstand much pressure. The English frontiersmen were on the prowl, backed by a colonial population much greater than that of their rivals.

King William lights the fuse

Nervously the French watched England's American colonies edge forward. Before the end of the 17th century they decided to check such growth before it became unmanageable. These were days of considerable uproar in England, and when in 1688 the Glorious Revolution fixed attention upon difficulties at home, the French made ready to strike. It was an opportunity not only to hurt the English colonies but also to humiliate the friends of the powerful Iroquois Indians. The ensuing conflict was known as King William's War. While it pitted England and France against each other in America, it was primarily European, for it was the accession of the Dutchman, William of Orange, to the English throne that touched off hostilities. His people already were fighting the French, and it was primarily his wish to involve England in the conflict that moved him to accept the throne.

Frenchmen in America welcomed the clash between the two European powers as an opportunity to conquer the English colonies, and in the winter of 1689–90, Count Louis de Frontenac, the governor of New France, lashed out at New York and New England. First his troops struck Schenectady, then the country between Maine and

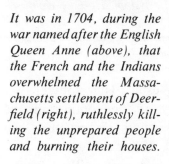

It was in 1704, during the war named after the English Queen Anne (above), that the French and the Indians overwhelmed the Massachusetts settlement of Deerfield (right), ruthlessly killing the unprepared people and burning their houses.

New Hampshire, and finally, Fort Loyal (the present Portland, Maine). Although New York was torn by rebellion against its own governor, common adversity drove the people in the Northern colonies together in defense. By May, 1690, a counterattack was launched that yielded up Port Royal in Acadia (now Nova Scotia) as a prize. During that summer Quebec itself was threatened but did not fall, and the war settled down to sporadic raids back and forth across the border. The Peace of Ryswick in 1697 required that each side return what it had captured; neither participant gained anything and no important questions were settled. An uncertain

126

peace ensued in Europe, but in America the French and English continued to spar. Shortly the gong would sound and round two would be under way.

War in the name of the queen

Within four years the European powers were fighting again. In 1700 the king of Spain died and was unforeseeing enough not to leave a direct heir. Sharp-eyed monarchs in other countries saw opportunity in this oversight and at once fell to battling over the successor, each hopeful of gaining an advantage. Louis XIV of France claimed the throne for his grandson and was at once opposed by England, Holland, Austria, and some of the German electorates that supported Leopold I, head of the Austrian house of Hapsburg. The conflict was properly labeled the War of the Spanish Succession, but in America the English honored their new sovereign by calling it Queen Anne's War. As most of Europe, as well as America, Asia, and Africa, was affected, the struggle was truly a world war. To most of the European nations who opposed France, it was a war to check the ambitions of Louis XIV, but to Holland and England it was a fight for colonies and commerce. During the years 1701 to 1713 the English concentrated their efforts on the American front in attempts to extinguish French claims on this side of the Atlantic.

American colonists received the news of more conflict with mixed feelings. Traders at Albany resented the development, for they had established a thriving business with Montreal, supplying the French with cheap trinkets for the Indians. So strong was their influence that a period of neutrality between New York and Canada existed during the early war years. Meanwhile the New England colonies, jealous over fishing rights off the Canadian banks and dissatisfied by their lack of gain in the previous war, enjoyed no peace. The French took advantage of friendship with the Indians and sent them against New England settlements without letup. The massacre at Deerfield, Massachusetts, in 1704, characterized the savagery of the coming struggle. Fifty-three killed and 111 prisoners was the high price the English paid in this raid. As the attacks increased, New Englanders asked the home government to conquer Canada as the only sure means of stopping the carnage. Accordingly, an expedition sailed against Port Royal in Acadia but accomplished nothing more than taking a few prisoners. In the following years attempts to storm the strongholds of New France were made both by land and sea with the same unsatisfactory results. Port Royal fell in 1710, as the British force outnumbering the French eight to one gained a rather empty victory. The next year another try was made, and a fleet carrying 12,000 men sailed to attack Quebec. Lost in a fog on the St. Lawrence River, the ships ran aground; 10 vessels and 900 men were the cost and not a blow was struck. Meanwhile the Spanish, now allied with the French, launched an attack from Florida and pressed the colony of South Carolina. The struggle in that sector saw the opponents so evenly matched that neither side won any decisive victories.

Peace breaks out again

In 1713, the Treaty of Utrecht ended the long struggle. France surrendered New Foundland and Acadia (except for Cape Breton Island) and all territory loosely described as Hudson Bay. France also recognized that the British were overlords of the powerful Iroquois. In a few years, however, the future looked a little less gloomy, and once more the French were hard at work empire-building. While the Treaty of Utrecht apparently gave a good deal to England, its terms were vague and territorial boundaries ill-defined. That knowledge was enough for her rivals; they dug furiously at the weak spots.

That the French were permanently undismayed by their American losses was made evident when they established the powerful Fort Louisbourg on Cape Breton. Located on an all-weather harbor, it stood poised to protect the residents of New France from naval invasion and to control

This flag, carried by New Englanders at Louisbourg in 1745, shows the symbol of England's military and naval power, Britannia, with spear and shield.

the northern fishing waters against all interlopers. So successful were the French in reviving their fishing industry that the Cape Breton region now prospered while New Foundland, recently lost to the English, declined.

The French wooed the Indians, sent their fur trappers plunging yet deeper into the American interior, and strove desperately to outsell English traders. Old posts in the Mississippi Valley, long in decay, were reactivated. If the English could not always see what was going on, they could feel it. Traders at places like Albany noticed that furs brought in by the Indians had declined sharply in quality; obviously the French were getting the best ones. The only answer to this was for the English to move farther west, into direct competition. It meant increased contact with the enemy, more friction, and renewed fighting. Despite that prospect, English traders surged forward and, encouraged by the Board of Trade at home, matched every move

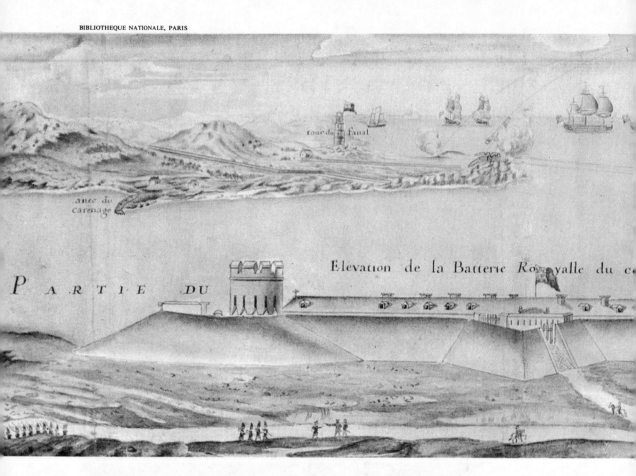

the French made. While trappers lived with the tribes, taking Indian wives and integrating with the natives to a degree not reached before, the Anglican church did its best to match the Jesuits by sending missionaries to work among the red men. When the mother countries would notify their colonial children that war was officially declared, the offspring would fly at each other with renewed vigor.

Captain Jenkins loses an ear

The Peace of Utrecht, like many other settlements, was only an armistice. Within 25 years Britain was again embroiled in war, and of course

her American colonies took part. The trouble arose out of England's commercial aggressiveness, this time in South America. While attempting to break into Spain's trading monopoly, an English seaman, Captain Robert Jenkins, asserted that one of his ears had been cut off by Spanish officials. Exhibiting in England what he said was the severed ear, Jenkins caused a wave of resentment against such a national insult. By the spring of 1739, an undisguisedly imperialistic war against Spain was on. After four years of inconclusive fighting, France sided with Spain. Meanwhile, over in the second ring of

130

The labels visible in the image: *Batterie de l'Isle Solennée*, *Isle Verte*, *Pointe a Rochefort*, *a terre*, *P O R T*

The Royal Battery (foreground) was captured by the British from the French early in the 1745 battle at Louisbourg, but the Island Battery (center, right) held out until the end. Its guns are shown dueling with those of the Americans (background).

the European circus, another war was raging as the king of Prussia tried to wrest territory from the Austrian Queen Maria Theresa. By 1744, the wars had merged into a single grand conflict. Spain, France, and Prussia were now pitted against Russia, Holland, England, and Austria. Known in Europe as the War of the Austrian Succession, its American counterpart was named in honor of England's King George.

To the American colonies, the main feature of the war was England's conquest of magnificent Fort Louisbourg. The action took place in the spring of 1745 when a fleet of 90 vessels out of Boston besieged the fortification. After 49 days, during which 9,000 cannonballs were hurled into it, the stronghold surrendered. Furious, the French dispatched a large fleet to recover their lost prize and, in retribution, to burn Boston. Bad weather combined with bad management led to a dismal failure. When still another attempt was made, the British sent the French squadrons fleeing for home.

Clearly, naval warfare was not going to save France her colonies.

A temporary peace resulted from the Treaty of Aix-la-Chapelle in 1748, by which England traded the newly captured Louisbourg for the port of Madras, India, recently taken by the French. American colonists complained loudly when their prize was handed over to ransom a place on the other side of the globe. Massachusetts had voted 50,000 pounds for the expedition against Louisbourg. Supplies and men had come from other New England colonies also. The home government's attempt to mollify them with money was a failure. Already Americans were having difficulty taking the international point of view.

In peace, prepare for war

With the return of peacetime conditions, the English became increasingly active in America. Men of the Hudson's Bay Company moved far out on the Northwestern plains, building posts and trading in an area the French regarded as their preserve. Louisbourg, now back in French hands, was flanked by a new and powerful English fort at Halifax to match military strength. Over in the Ohio Valley the contest reached new proportions. While the English constantly strengthened their position, the French answered by building a series of forts around Lake Erie and on the Allegheny River. Governor Robert Dinwiddie of Virginia sent young George Washington in 1753 to order out the interlopers, but they politely ignored him. The angry governor next dispatched Captain William Trent to build a post where the Allegheny and Monongahela Rivers joined to form the Ohio, and he was *not* ignored; the French threw him out and built Fort Duquesne. Once more Washington marched westward; this time he defeated the French and built Fort Necessity. But in 1754 the enemy captured it. With the outposts of the two nations in constant friction, enough heat was being generated to start another conflagration.

That the English were not yet ready for war was indicated by their offer to accept the Allegheny Mountains as their western boundary. All they wanted was part of Nova Scotia in return. Strangely, the French refused, and with the failure of diplomacy, the return to arms was inevitable. Despite peaceful efforts, both sides had long expected another war, and during the summer of 1754, active preparations were made. Meanwhile, representatives of seven English colonies, along with those of the Iroquois, met at Albany to work out plans for their mutual defense when hostilities were renewed. It was no spontaneous meeting. The English government sponsored it, at the request of the Board of Trade, with the hope of organizing all Indians south of the Great Lakes. The Iroquois were unhappy because they were not supported enough in their forays against the French. And what was worse, while the Indians were helping the English, the Virginians were stealing their lands.

The conference produced a plan for intercolonial organization, drawn up by Benjamin Franklin, known as the Albany Plan of Union. It proposed a "super colony," loyal to England but organized to simplify colonial administration and lend unity of effort. The proposal was unanimously adopted by the Albany Congress and unanimously rejected by the colonies involved. Despite such sharp disapproval, the notion of the Albany Plan was significant, for it recognized the need for American union, a thought that was to return to colonial minds within the next few years.

While the delegates debated at Albany, news of Fort Necessity's loss was received. The English wasted no more time in discussion; they sent General Edward Braddock to America with two regiments of redcoats. After a laborious journey through the wilderness, plagued by sickness and hard marching, Braddock's forces met the enemy in July, 1755, near Fort Duquesne. There the French and Indians, using the natural protection of trees and fighting guerrilla-style, slashed at the English forces until they were cut to pieces. With Braddock mortally wounded

General Edward Braddock, commander in the battle for Fort Duquesne in 1755, was shot through the lungs near the end of the struggle with the French and Indians and, as his army retreated, was carried for two days before he died.

This sketch of James Wolfe, made in 1759 at Quebec by an officer, George Townshend, is thought to be the best likeness of him.

and many of his troops dead or badly wounded, the long march home began. During that summer Governor William Shirley of Massachusetts led a similar expedition against Fort Niagara, only to be hurled back. The English now made ready in earnest. Seven thousand Acadians, now under their rule but considered a risk because of their French origin, were evacuated from their homes in Nova Scotia and scattered along the Eastern and Southern seaboard. Although their European parents were still at peace, the colonies in America were poised for an all-out struggle. In May of 1756, the starting signal was given in Europe and the Seven Years War was under way there. The American part of it was called the French and Indian War.

Seven fateful years

As usual, the European conflict arose out of jealousies and a struggle for power. Austria still had lingering grievances against Prussia from the previous war. As she plotted alliances against Prussia, that country turned to England for support. France promptly signed on with Austria, and the stage was set. In America, where preliminary sparring had gone on for two years, the principals were more than ready. The opening rounds of the main event were punishing ones for the English. In Europe, Frederick II of Prussia staggered under the combined blows of France, Russia, and Austria while the French won some sparkling engagements at sea. In the Western Hemisphere, French hopes rose as General Louis Joseph de Montcalm took command in Canada and chopped away at northern colonial outposts of England. These reverses, along with others in India, posed a serious problem for the British government and made it clear that some drastic reforms in military strategy must be carried out if there was to be any hope of victory in this international war.

The tide began to turn in 1757. William Pitt, the Great Commoner,

134

On July 26, 1758, English soldiers rowed into Louisbourg harbor and captured two French frigates guarding the fortress. One ship was taken (right), the other burned. For the second time, Louisbourg surrendered to the English.

took command of the British war effort and turned all his energies toward the pressing problems at hand. At home he engaged in a house cleaning that saw a number of older and less aggressive generals replaced by young and ambitious officers. Pulling out of the Continental theater as much as he could, Pitt focused his attention upon the American scene. By the following year young Major General Jeffrey Amherst and Brigadier General James Wolfe had recaptured the great Canadian fort of Louisbourg, opening the way to the St. Lawrence Valley. Colonials in America were made more enthusiastic for the war by an increased recognition of their military men, a policy that considerably strengthened campaigning English forces.

By 1759, all was ready for a gigantic three-pronged assault upon the Canadian French. In this, "the wonderful year," the war was won as Wolfe moved against Quebec by way of the St. Lawrence River, and Amherst plunged toward the same objective by way of Lake Champlain, while a third contingent captured Fort Niagara. On the night of Sep-

135

tember 12, Wolfe put ashore 5,000 troops who, after scaling the heights before Quebec by night, stood ready for the final assault on the Plains of Abraham next morning. In a historic battle both Wolfe and Montcalm lost their lives, but victory went to the English. Five days later the city of Quebec surrendered. Only Montreal, the last French stronghold, remained; it 'fell during the next year. With that surrender, in the autumn of 1760, the British gained practical control of all Canada.

France wanted to make peace. But she had commitments to her European allies, who opposed treating on that subject with England. Maria Theresa of Austria wanted her hated enemy Frederick II of Prussia crushed, and as the French troops were carrying on a fairly successful, though expensive, campaign against the Prussians, she wanted to continue the war. France now turned to Spain and convinced Charles III, who had recently come to power, that England ought not to dominate the North American scene. By the Family Compact that followed, the Spanish entered the war against the English in 1761. Pitt now became thoroughly stubborn about peace talks and pushed the war effort until he forced his opponents to give up the struggle. France lost West Indian bases; Spain lost Havana and Manila. By the end of 1762, they were willing to listen to Pitt's proposals.

The rewards and costs of war

When the diplomats gathered at Paris in February, 1763, to make peace, significant changes were in the offing. At one stroke France gave up an empire when it signed over Canada to the English. Another huge slice of land was fully surrendered as she gave up any further claim to territory between the Alleghenies and the Mississippi River. Spain, once again helping the French Bourbons fight their wars, paid the price of involvement by surrendering Florida and any rights she had east of the Mississippi in order to regain Cuba. The French regained the sugar islands of Martinique, Guadeloupe, and St. Lucia, but as far as North America was concerned, they were forever finished.

Because of the territory she gained, both in America and elsewhere, Great Britain emerged as the most powerful nation in the world. Henceforth her westward movement across America was to be unhindered by any other European power. American colonists, eager to expand and to speculate in Western lands, looked upon this development with great anticipation. When they discovered that Mother England had other plans for the newly acquired territory, their happiness turned to sullen gloom. But the leaders of England, intoxicated by their country's meteoric rise to wealth and power, did not hear the mutterings across the Atlantic.

METROPOLITAN MUSEUM OF ART

Bruton Parish Church, in 18th-century Williamsburg, painted by Woodworth Thompson.

LIFE IN
COLONIAL AMERICA

From the forests of Maine to the marshes of Georgia, the men and women who immigrated to America pursued the great lure of the New World—equality of opportunity. Some stayed along the coast, where the Atlantic, an abundant fishing ground and the passageway to the rich markets of Europe, brought them wealth. Here, working in the growing cities of Boston, New York, Philadelphia, and Charleston, tradesmen prospered and artisans found outlets for their talents. Others drifted inland, attracted by the soil that was theirs if their courage was great and their backs strong. From the wilderness they carved farms and homesteads that became the foundations of villages and towns. In the South, vast plantations based on slavery, an incongruous element of colonial life, grew and flourished. There were sharp differences in the ways of life, the philosophies, and the governments of the various colonies. But united by common problems and swept on by the tide of common successes, colonists of different nationalities were transformed into a new breed—Americans.

COLONIAL TYPES

COLLECTION OF NATHANIEL HAMLEN

Among the leading citizens of aristo-cratic Charleston was Ralph Izard, a wealthy Huguenot planter. The double portrait (above) of Izard and his wife was painted in 1775 by John Singleton Copley.

The adultlike Sunday-best clothing of Pilgrim and Puritan youngsters is seen in the painting of the sober-faced Mason children (left) done around 1670 by an unknown artist in Massachusetts.

The Quaker settlers were persecuted and harassed in New England and New York. But men and women like those painted by Nicolino Calyo (right) later found free-dom of worship in early Pennsylvania.

Baltimore was just a village when the picture above was painted in 1752. By 1776, however, it was a busy seaport and the ninth-largest city in the colonies.

The center of Boston's commercial district was State Street (right). It was in front of the Old State House (center) that the Boston Massacre took place.

The South's most prosperous port was Charleston (below), where ships were loaded with profitable cargoes of indigo and rice from the inland plantations.

CENTERS OF COMMERCE

A NEW METROPOLIS

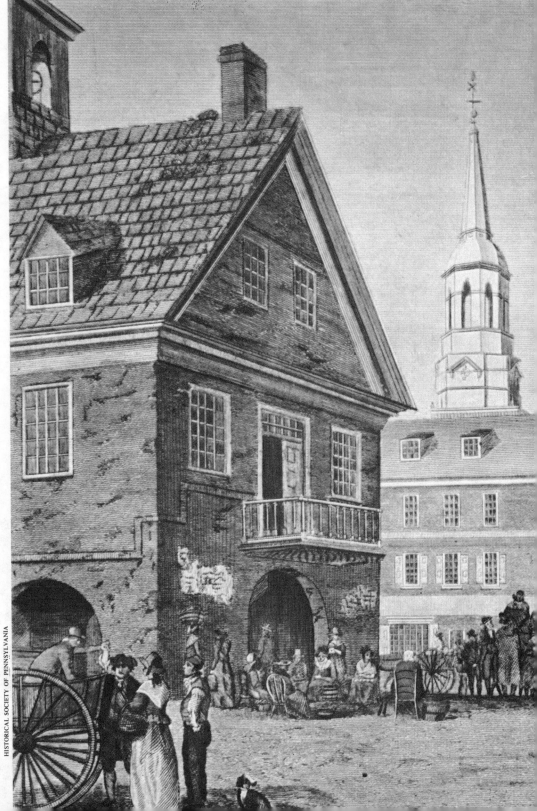

The most enterprising and attractive of the 18th-century American cities was bustling Philadelphia. The heart of it was the junction of Second and High Streets, marked by the spire of Christ Church. Distances to other cities were measured from this intersection, shown below in an engraving from a 1799 series by Thomas Birch.

THE BOUNTIFUL OCEAN

Along the New England coast, where fishing and trade provided jobs and income for thousands, a powerful and wealthy merchant class came into being. Cod fishing, which had brought European fishermen to New Foundland and New England waters in the past, was now a lucrative industry in the colonies. The drawing at the right, made around 1720, illustrates how the cod were caught, cleaned on large stages, salted, and dried for sale after the valuable oil had been removed from the livers of the fish. (See legend at the top.)

Merchant John Amory, above in a Copley portrait, made a fortune in Boston but left America when the Revolution began. The great success of the colonial mariners angered their British competitors, who insisted that Parliament tighten restrictions on New World commerce.

Yankee seamen, like the one at the right from *A Book of Trades, or Library of Useful Arts,* protested loudly when the English attempted to limit their activities. The result was downright evasion of the law, through smuggling or other means, and a stiffening of resistance to the crown.

NEW YORK PUBLIC LIBRARY

MUSEUM OF FINE ARTS, BOSTON

View of a Stage & also of $\check{y}$ manner of Fishing for, Curing & Drying Cod at NEW FOUND LAND. A. The Habit of $\check{y}$ Fishermen. B. The Line. C. The manner of Fishing. D. The Dressers of $\check{y}$ Fish. E. The Trough into which they throw $\check{y}$ Cod when Dressed. F. Salt Boxes. G. The manner of Carrying $\check{y}$ Cod. H. The Cleansing $\check{y}$ Cod. I. A Press to extract $\check{y}$ Oyl from $\check{y}$ Cods Livers. K. Casks to receive $\check{y}$ Water & Blood that comes from $\check{y}$ Livers. L. Another Cask to receive $\check{y}$ Oyl. M. The manner of Drying $\check{y}$ Cod.

A. DEVANEY

This "sacred cod" carving hangs in the Massachusetts State House.

145

Indians and British soldiers are among the guests depicted in the painting, *Colonial Wedding in Virginia* (above). Ladies and bewigged gentlemen wave farewell to the departing newly-weds, while the bride's mother sobs into her handkerchief and Indians watch impassively.

TOBACCO FOR ENGLAND

Virginia's prosperity was based on tobacco and was therefore dependent on
the slaves who worked in the fields. In
this old water color (left), the slaves
dance and relax during a work respite.

The 1784 drawing (right) pictures a
wharf where tobacco was loaded for shipment abroad. For years tobacco was better
than money in Virginia, and Church of
England ministers drew their salary in it.

THE GREAT PLANTATIONS

The half-century before the Revolution was the Golden Age of Virginia. Planters lived elegantly on their tidewater estates, which encompassed thousands of acres. The plantation shown here consisted of a great house, slave cabins, barns, warehouses, and a water mill.

CHAPTER 6

SEEDS OF REVOLUTION

When the sounds of cannonading in the Seven Years War died away, there was revealed along the Atlantic seaboard a new nationality. For more than a century an American strain had been developing, so imperceptibly that many in America as well as the Old World were unaware of it. Only when England tried to exercise increased control did the colonists realize that an individual society, ready to demand more freedom, had arisen. The war itself had not only awakened them to their potentialities, but its result had freed them from fear of the French and Spanish. Only the Indians stood between them and unlimited expansion. It is little wonder that they began to flex their biceps and assert themselves. In some respects, the American Revolution had started.

For some years England's tightening restrictions had annoyed the colonists. To strike out at her commercial rivals, England had introduced a series of laws known as

King George III, English ruler during the American Revolution, as he appeared in his coronation robes. Painted by Allan Ramsay.

the Navigation Acts. They conformed to the prevailing economic theory of Europe called mercantilism. Commercially active Continental countries acquired as much bullion as possible through trade, particularly with their own colonies, over which they had complete control. They strengthened themselves with this treasure and often used it to finance wars against their neighbors. It was with the same idea of making their empire self-sufficient that the British turned toward mercantilism.

The first act, passed in 1650, was designed primarily to curb the Dutch, who had captured a large portion of the carrying trade. All foreign vessels were forbidden to trade with the English colonies. Within a year the law was tightened to force goods from the colonies into English vessels only. Ten years later, in 1660, and again in 1663, additional provisions stated that not only were all foreign merchants excluded from the English colonies, but certain "enumerated" goods, like sugar, cotton, indigo, and tobacco, must be transported to England before they could be sold elsewhere. By a law of 1673, ships bound for England from the colonies, bearing any of the enumerated goods, were required to post a bond to insure delivery of the goods in an English port as promised. The law also required that duties be paid at the point of shipment. These acts were crowned by the statute of 1696, which tightened the existing laws to the extreme. Henceforth no colonial goods might be carried from one colony to another except in English-built ships. Governors were threatened with heavy fines for allowing infractions, and any colonial laws that conflicted with the act were declared null and void. The better to enforce its edict, the English government now separated the American colonies into two admiralty divisions and appointed judges to each to deal with violators. This final attempt must have been effective, for at once trade between the colonies and England soared.

The Navigation Acts, although aimed at the Dutch, were enacted also to assure English traders a monopoly in America. The Northern colonies were those most interested in trade, and they welcomed the acts of 1650–51, for the Dutch were their chief competitors. Under the law, vessels of New England were regarded as English, and as the mother country did not have enough ships to carry the products herself, colonial shipowners gladly supplied the remainder. New England quickly became an active trading center, and its merchants engaged in direct commerce with European nations, blandly ignoring the restrictive acts of 1660 and 1663, and shipping enumerated goods when and where they pleased. Only extreme internal dissension and warfare at home kept England from enforcing her commercial laws.

England's restrictive legislation, though often ignored by the colonists, served to drive the two societies apart. Laws demanding that an American merchant first bring his goods to England before selling them elsewhere could be evaded. But when the home government closed its markets to American agricultural products, there were no means of trading oats, wheat, beef, or bacon for English hardware or textiles. Although the colonials were forbidden to manufacture, this kind of legislation forced them to it. Short-sighted Englishmen could not see that with a plentiful supply of iron, wool, and wood, the Americans could easily turn to the production of manufactured articles. English restrictive legislation merely hastened the process and inadvertently pushed Americans toward self-sufficiency.

Imperial England's new discipline

At the Peace of Paris in 1763, England found that she had taken a gigantic leap forward as a world power and colonizer. Problems of administration and control over this

To enforce the Sugar Act, Parliament ruled that colonial merchants accused of smuggling were to be tried in the admiralty courts in Halifax, Nova Scotia.

global domain now put her in a serious mood; no longer would haphazard methods suffice to run the imperial firm. A glance at the exchequer revealed that the national debt had almost doubled since Braddock marched toward Fort Duquesne. Taxation in England had mounted steadily, and new sources of income were becoming scarce. Why not ask the colonials for financial help? Large amounts had been spent in their defense, and more would be needed to protect them in the future against the Indians. To this the colonists objected. In their opinion, they had already contributed rather heavily and were then in debt about 750,000 pounds. If wages and profits were counted, the colonies annually contributed 2,000,000 pounds to England in addition to taxes. To them, it seemed enough. The English government was not to be put off, however. Money was needed, and it must be forthcoming. Orders went out to stiffen the customs collections, make the much-disobeyed Molasses Act of 1733 effective, extend stamp duties to America, further restrain colonial manufacturing, add more enumerated goods to the list of exports from America, and forbid colonials to issue paper money. These ideas were not hatched suddenly. Government officials had deliberated upon future fiscal requirements. In 1763, the ministry asked the Board of Trade a series of questions about the more efficient operation of the

The Stamp Act of 1765 brought a violent reaction from Americans. In the woodcut above, a group of New Hampshire citizens hangs a stamp agent in effigy. At the left is an engraving from a 1794 German almanac that gives the strong reaction of a group of patriots in Boston who burned the stamps. At the right is the stamp that caused the trouble.

empire. These concerned the type of government best suited to colonies, the number of soldiers necessary for adequate protection, the amounts of money that ought to be expected from the colonies for such protection, and finally, how best could England gain profit from her new territorial acquisitions.

The general result of this study was the Proclamation of 1763. It recommended that the "civilized" part of the new territory be given governments similar to those of the earlier colonies. Accordingly, Canada, East Florida, and West Florida now came into the colonial sphere. "Uncivilized" portions, such as Indian country lying west of the Appalachians, were to be reserved for the aborigines; only licensed traders could deal with them. By the drawing of this imaginary line between the settled and unsettled parts of the colonies, many a hopeful American speculator was cut off from what he thought would be a lucrative investment in land. Over loud objections, the English nevertheless fixed the line, hoping to check the westward movement until the government thought expansion both safe and wise. Officials were soon to learn, as did those of the United States later on, that the Americans were not to be fenced in. No set of laws would ever be devised to check the surging frontiersmen; they broke them as a matter of course.

More laws to break

Other recommendations made to the ministry resulted in specific financial legislation designed to produce greater revenues. In 1764 the Sugar Act was passed. Although it lowered the duty rates set in 1733, under the Molasses Act, it provided extensive regulations concerning collection. Ship captains had to post bonds to insure delivery of their cargoes, and illicit trade was to be ferreted out and stopped. Americans had no objection to the *passage* of such legislation, but they were incensed to think that the government planned to *enforce* it. Smuggling had become a time-honored calling along the Atlantic seacoast, and now it was in jeopardy.

During recent wars colonials had issued paper money, which had decreased in value. Debtors in America attempted to pay off their obligations in England with this money, and thus actually avoid payment of the entire amount. The Currency Act of 1764 put a stop to the issuance of fiat money and presented Americans with the problems of paying Englishmen what they owed in coin of the realm. Angered, the colonials resolved to buy less in England and to use products made at home. The seriousness of this intent is seen in the vow of Yale College students to buy no more imported liquors; henceforth they would patronize home industry only.

The Stamp Act of 1765 is another example of the attempt to raise more money in the colonies. Revenue stamps had to be bought for legal documents issued in America, or for the sale of such items as dice, playing cards, newspapers, calendars, and almanacs. The act roused heated opposition, despite England's claim that the taxes would be put into a defense chest for the colonies. Many who sympathized with England's financial distress complained that a new and unfair principle was involved. It was one thing to tax imperial commerce, but quite another to levy against items wholly American.

Even before news of the Stamp Act reached America, another disturbing piece of legislation was foisted upon the colonials. Called the Quartering Act, it required civil authorities to provide barracks and supplies for British soldiers. The government felt that the number of troops to be sent across the Atlantic would far exceed the available military quarters. New Yorkers saw at once that they would be hard hit, for the British army's North American headquarters was in their colony. So disproportionate would be the load that the legislature refused to carry out certain provisions of the act. Word was sent to the governor from England that he was to sign no laws until the legislators yielded. After a stalemate lasting several months, the New Yorkers gave in. But they did not forget that they had been forced, and resentment against the British government ran high.

Mob action

As restrictive laws rained down upon them, the colonists reacted with rage and violence. Individuals spontaneously banded together, and mob action was the order of the day. During the summer of 1765, young men calling themselves Sons of Liberty roamed the streets of Boston jeering at British officials and looking for trouble. In August, a mob entered the office of the admiralty court's deputy registrar, burned his records, and proceeded to the wine cellar of another customs official. After sampling liberally of his royal wares, "being enflam'd with Rum & Wine . . . [they] proceeded with Shouts to the Dwelling House of the Hon-l. Thos. Hutchinson, Esq., Lieut. Governor, & enter'd in a voyalent manner." As the invaders broke down the lieutenant governor's front door with axes, the startled official jumped from his supper table and fled to the shouts of "Damn him, he's upstairs. We'll have him yet!" By morning the house was burned out, its walls partly caved in, and a section of the roof gone. The rioters had melted into the population, and the government's offer of a reward for their delivery was never claimed.

Perhaps it was more than patriotism, heightened by libations in the wine cellar, that fired up the zealots. In nearby Rhode Island, young women had notified the world that they would refuse the attentions of any man who voiced approval of the Stamp Act. Such a powerful interdict was bound to have its influence. Those who were unconcerned over the embargo on affections found excitement in mass meetings, parading, and shouting general disapproval of authority. The feeling was infectious, and even conservatives decided that under such a serious threat to their liberties they were "not averse to a little rioting."

The rights of Englishmen

Widespread protest over England's restrictive legislation was not confined to house-wrecking and window-smashing. The General Court of Massachusetts officially protested, saying that the Sugar Act would ruin the New England fisheries. Molasses, from the Caribbean islands, was an important part of the triangular trade the merchants carried on, and the new tax promised to hurt that thriving commerce. To Bostonians like Samuel Adams, the Sugar Act was more than an English economic measure; it threatened colonial political liberties. If trade could be taxed, then why could not everything the colonials had be taxed? This meant an end to self-government, guaranteed by many a colonial charter.

Virginians felt the same appre-

After the repeal of the noxious Stamp Act in 1766, this English print shows government members as a mournful group carrying the dead act to its grave.

hensions. In May, 1765, legislators at Williamsburg registered a sharp objection known as the Virginia Resolves. Twenty-nine-year-old Patrick Henry presented the resolutions, and after listening to his impassioned oratory, in which cries of "Treason" were heard among the listeners, the House of Burgesses reluctantly approved. In general the resolutions were a recitation of the rights of Englishmen, from the time of the first American settlement, and an insistence that those rights had been transferred to these shores with the immigrants. Foremost in the heritage, the most inalienable among the rights, was the privilege of being taxed by one's own representatives. As for Virginia, Henry held that its legislators, locally elected, were the only ones with the right to tax their people.

Word of the action spread up and down the seacoast. The Virginia Resolves were thought by New Yorkers to be too treasonable for publication, but New Englanders had no such

157

George Grenville (left) as prime minister pushed through the Stamp Act; Charles Rockingham (center), his successor, repealed it; and Charles Townshend (right), a later chancellor of the exchequer, created new colonial taxes.

qualms. By June they appeared in a Newport paper and shortly thereafter in several Boston newspapers. Sir Francis Bernard, governor of Massachusetts, said that at first he thought the people would submit to the Stamp Act but that the publishing of the Virginia Resolves "proved an Alarum-bell to the disaffected." John Adams went further. He said that to the author of the resolutions went credit for starting the American Revolution.

The Stamp Act Congress

The Resolves surprised New Englanders. Virginia, the Old Dominion, was regarded as the most loyal of His Majesty's colonies and the least likely to be disobedient. For the moment, the Southerners appeared to have taken the initiative, and not to be outdone in patriotism, the General Court of Massachusetts now

asked for delegates from all colonies to meet at New York in October to consider resistance to the Stamp Act. There was only a weak response, and four of the colonies, including Virginia, did not even send anyone to the Stamp Act Congress. Its members agreed that Englishmen in America had the same rights as those in England and could not be taxed without their consent. They protested against the system of trying violators without juries in the admiralty courts. All Englishmen, they said, had the right of trial by their peers. The gathering of delegates, from South Carolina to Massachusetts, indicated that despite their mild approach there was a growing community of sentiment, and that out of the crucible of common grievance there would emerge a new people. For the first time, a genuinely representative convention of the American colonies had acted in unison.

England backs down

Early in 1766, Parliament repealed the Stamp Act. It was not because its members were cowed by violence from across the Atlantic or by insistence upon rights. Aside from the fact that officials experienced a nightmare of confusion and non-cooperation in trying to make collections, there were increasing complaints from English merchants that business was declining. Colonials had resolved not to import from the mother country until some of her legislation was rescinded, and the result was noticeable. Within 20 months exports to America fell off by half. George III was at the same time tiring of his prime minister, George Grenville, who constantly lectured him about his responsibilities and otherwise annoyed him. While the king floundered, Parliament moved toward repeal. One of its members, a merchant, got to the root of the matter when he wrote to Lord Charles Rockingham, who had succeeded Grenville, "Our trade is hurt; what the devil have you been doing? For our part, we don't pretend to understand your politics and American matters, but our trade is hurt; pray remedy it, and plague you if you won't." By March, 1766,

In 1767, Benjamin Franklin had this cartoon made and sent to his friends. It prophesies the plight of England with her American colonies cut off.

The BLOODY MASSACRE perpetrated in King——Street BOSTON on March 5th 1770 by a party of the 29th REGT

Engrav'd Printed & Sold by PAUL REVERE BOSTON

Unhappy Boston! see thy Sons deplore,
Thy hallow'd Walks besmear'd with guiltless Gore:
While faithless P——n and his savage Bands,
With murd'rous Rancour stretch their bloody Hands;
Like fierce Barbarians grinning o'er their Prey,
Approve the Carnage, and enjoy the Day.

If scalding drops from Rage from Anguish Wrung,
If speechless Sorrows lab'ring for a Tongue,
Or if a weeping World can ought appease
The plaintive Ghosts of Victims such as these;
The Patriot's copious Tears for each are shed,
A glorious Tribute which embalms the Dead.

But know, Fate summons to that awful Goal,
Where Justice strips the Murd'rer of his Soul
Should venal C——ts the scandal of the Land,
Snatch the relentless Villain from her Hand.
Keen Execrations on this Plate inscrib'd,
Shall reach a Judge who never can be brib'd.

The unhappy Sufferers were Messr_s SAML GRAY, SAML MAVERICK, JAMS CALDWELL, CRISPUS ATTUCKS & PATR CARR
Killed. Six wounded, two of them (CHRISTR MONK & JOHN CLARK) Mortally

S.G. S.M. J.C. C.J.A. P.C.

Paul Revere's engraving of the Boston Massacre of 1770 was colonial propaganda. It claimed seven men were killed; actually five Americans lost their lives. The five coffins, drawn by Revere, were used on broadsides about the dead patriots.

a remedy was found; the act was rescinded.

Townshend and his duties

To no one's great surprise, William Pitt succeeded Rockingham as prime minister, but to the astonishment of many, including the recipient, Charles Townshend received the appointment as chancellor of the exchequer. Those who had hoped he would have only minor influence in the government were further dismayed when shortly Pitt was incapacitated by illness and Townshend became the power behind the scenes. As a member of Parliament, he had voted for both the passage and the repeal of the Stamp Act; now he veered once more and announced he was in favor of the act after all. Early in 1767, at the consideration of the budget, he assented to a proposal that would tax the colonies heavily so that levies against English landholders might be reduced. Members of the House of Commons, many of whom were property owners, expressed pleasure when he described how additional revenues could be gained by tightening customs regulations in America and laying on additional duties. His Revenue Act of June laid a tonnage tax on all vessels entering colonial ports and applied duties to such manufactures as glass, painters' lead, and paper, as well as tea. During the same month another act ordered the reorganization of the American cus-

John Adams defended British soldiers tried for murder for their part in the Boston Massacre. Portrait, Charles Willson Peale.

toms service and the creation of additional admiralty courts. This last piece of legislation particularly infuriated the Americans, who continued to insist upon trials by jury.

Vox populi and violence

Townshend, who died before the Revenue Act became effective, probably would have been surprised to hear the abuse piled upon his head for his program. He might have been flattered to learn that the principal objection to it by the colonials was that it worked. Smuggling came almost to a halt and customs revenues soared. One of those affected was John Hancock, a well-known Boston shipper, who paid little attention and no money to the authorities who demanded duty payments on the wine he imported. When his sloop *Liberty* was seized for nonpayment of customs, officials were roughly handled by angry crowds, their houses stormed, and one of their small boats carried triumphantly to Boston Commons, where it was burned. Incidents such as this caused England to send more officials as well as additional troops.

Day after day the tension mounted. Finally, on the evening of March 5, 1770, the inevitable occurred. A false fire alarm had drawn many people out into the streets, and as the mob surged back and forth, one of its members hurled a snowball at one of the stiff-backed British sentries. After being hit several times, he called for aid and got it. The angry crowd now moved closer, clubs were swung, a soldier was knocked down, shots were fired, and then in the shocked silence that followed, Bostonians saw five of their own lying dead or dying.

On September 30, 1768, a British fleet, shown in the engraving below by Paul Revere, anchored in Boston harbor. The next day soldiers of the 14th and 19th Regiments debarked at the Long Wharf and marched up King Street.

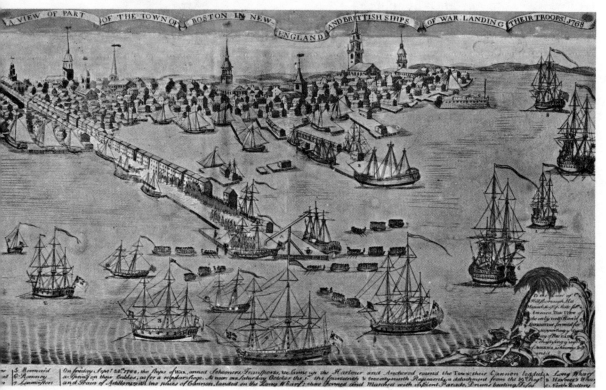

In 1774, Samuel Adams used some private government letters to incite rebellion. Benjamin Franklin was held responsible, and he was arraigned in England by the Privy Council (above) for allowing the letters to become public.

History would record it as a massacre. The affair might have attracted only short-lived attention had it not been for the artful way in which Samuel Adams fanned the flames of fury at a town meeting. So great was the effect of his oratory that Governor Thomas Hutchinson acceded to

163

his demand that British troops be withdrawn from the city of Boston to islands in the harbor.

Although Lord North had addressed the House of Commons concerning partial repeal of the Townshend duties on the very day of the Boston Massacre, events had moved too far for such belated apologies to satisfy Americans. Months before blood was shed, it became clear to them that England proposed legislative interference as well as stricter economic control in the colonies. In 1768, the Massachusetts assembly circularized other colonies on the question of joint action against the home government for its invasion of their rights. Several legislatures passed acts of condemnation, some of which were based on the Virginia Resolves of 1769. Men like John Dickinson, who wrote a series of letters purportedly by a Pennsylvania farmer, contributed to a united sense of resentment. His writings were read in all parts of the colonies. In the weeks that followed the Boston Massacre, Samuel Adams provided some organization to the letter writers by setting up Committees of Correspondence. The plan was designed to provide nearby towns with information about the progress of events in Boston, but it soon was used as a model in neighboring colonies. Ultimately it would itself become an instrument of revolution, spreading news, assisting in intercolonial organization, and laying a

groundwork for new governments.

Angered colonials did more than write letters to each other about their rising discontent. They remembered that nonimportation of goods had resulted in the repeal of the Stamp Act, and they now applied the same pressure to the Townshend Acts. Merchants organized associations pledged not to import any goods that might be taxed by Parliament to raise revenue in America. Although members of Parliament insisted they were not responding to pressure, they shortly repealed the duties on

Abraham Whipple (left) was one of the Providence merchants who destroyed the British schooner Gaspee *(above) in 1772. During the Revolution, he was a privateer and once captured 10 British ships in 10 successive nights.*

lead, glass, and paper. To maintain the principle of taxing the colonies, however, they retained the tax on tea, feeling that this would harm no one. Americans were happy that their embargo had once again forced England to retreat, but the method was not without cost. Nonimportation meant a rise in the price of goods already in America, and the consumer often paid heavily for his patriotism.

The partial repeal of the Townshend Acts in 1770 proved to be a temporary sop. Merchants were happy over a restoration of normal business relationships, and conservatives were relieved that another crisis had passed. Restless souls like Sam Adams grew discouraged. No one seemed excited about the cause of personal liberty any more. But just when Adams feared that the spirit of resistance was dying, Lieutenant William Dudingston of His Majesty's customs schooner *Gaspee* came to the rescue.

Rhode Islanders, of independent mind from the start, greatly resented British interference with their smuggling. One June afternoon in 1772,

Dudingston ran the *Gaspee* aground on a sandspit off Providence. That night about 150 colonials forced him and his men to go ashore and burned his vessel to the waterline. Dudingston was wounded trying to save the *Gaspee*.

English authorities were in a rage over the daring action—a rage compounded by the fact that in two trials at Newport, no culprits could be produced and not a shred of evidence could be turned up because of the unitedly hostile Rhode Islanders. And as if this were not bad enough, men like Patrick Henry and Thomas Jefferson, in the Virginia House of Burgesses, challenged England's right to hold court in Rhode Island. Such impudence stung the British into further restrictive legislation.

Tea time

In a bill passed in 1773, the House of Commons tried to rescue the East India Company from holding a surplus of 17,000,000 pounds of tea. Permission was given the company to send tea directly to America, free of all duties and customs in England and subject to only a threepenny tax in America. The company was now able to sell its tea in America more cheaply than its competitors. Although Americans had paid a tea duty for six years without much grumbling, they now objected to the levy and more particularly to the advantage given to the East India Company. Even worse,

many American merchants were denied appointments to sell the company's tea, and such appointments were given to English favorites.

Without notifying anyone in America, the company sent small shipments of tea to various Atlantic ports. At Charleston it was quietly stored away, and at New York and Philadelphia the boxes were placed in vessels returning to England. British customs officials, aware of public sentiment, elected to make no trouble. But at Boston, events took a different turn. When the news got out that ships bearing tea had arrived, placards calling it a "detestable plague" and announcing that "the hour of destruction . . . stares you in the face" appeared on buildings. As many as 2,000 citizens protested at public gatherings, to no avail; Governor Hutchinson (who had two sons and a nephew among the consignees) was bound that the tea be landed. His decision was quickly answered. On December 16 a band of "Indians" clambered aboard the vessels and under the approving glances of Bostonians threw chests of tea worth 15,000 pounds over the rail. Although the imported tea, tax included, was sold to Americans for less than Englishmen at home had to pay, the

The British image of America in 1774 is shown in this cartoon. A group looking like hoodlums, having tarred and feathered an excise man and forced him to drink tea, appears to plan hanging him from a tree.

167

On December 16, 1773, 150 thinly disguised Boston patriots boarded English ships and dumped 342 chests of tea into the harbor. An 1846 print by N. Currier.

administration of the levy, and the theory behind it, irritated colonials. This violent action deeply angered Lord North and his associates, who regarded such conduct as a flouting of constituted authority.

Reaction from the government was prompt and drastic. In March, 1774, Lord North asked Parliament to take steps to fasten discipline more firmly on the colonies. The prime minister made it clear that the gauntlet had been thrown down by the Americans and severe punishment was called for. General Thomas Gage thought four regiments would suffice; Parliament answered with four coercive acts. The first closed the Port of Boston. The Massachusetts Government Act revoked the colony's charter and placed its administrative officers directly under royal control. An Administration of Justice Act provided that any British official charged with a capital offense in putting down a riot or collecting revenue should be sent to England for trial. (because of the known hostility of the colonial bench and bar). A fourth law revived the Quartering Act of 1765, but this time it said that *occupied* buildings might be used to house troops. Additionally, there was the Quebec Act, extending Canada's boundary to the Ohio River and taking over an area in which Virginia, Connecticut, and Massachusetts all had claims. When these laws had been put into effect, George III remarked, "The die is now cast; the colonies must either submit or triumph." For a monarch whose opinions were not always sound, this was prophetic.

The opposition unites

Colonial irritations had steadily mounted for some time. Scattered incidents had caused anger, but there was no compelling motive for all-out resistance. The coercive acts pulled the trigger. In September delegates from every colony except Georgia met at Philadelphia determined to offer united resistance. After they had adopted a declaration of rights, they got down to the more practical aspects of their business. They formed a Continental Association pledged to enforce nonimportation of any English goods. Although the delegates from Massachusetts were in a mood of violence—and probably agreed with Patrick Henry, who announced that "Government is dissolved . . . We are in a state of nature"—most of those present were not yet ready for

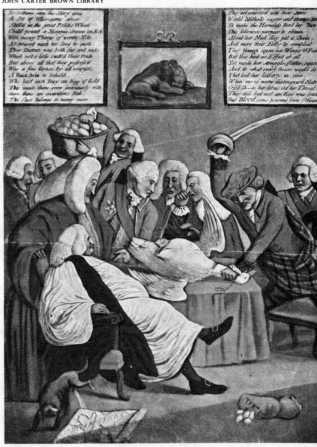

English ministers kill the goose—meant to be American—that lays the golden eggs.

revolution. At the moment they were principally interested in resistance to what they believed to be a violation of their rights as Englishmen and resolved to fight against coercion. When cooperation in this resolve was assured, they adjourned, and agreed that they would meet again the next May, if still coerced.

By that time shots had been fired and blood let, and whether the colonists liked it or not, the Revolution was under way.

MAIN TEXT CONTINUES IN VOLUME 3

The Pilgrim and Puritan Fathers

A SPECIAL CONTRIBUTION BY

A. L. ROWSE

The early founders of America, men of strong faith and convictions, came from England and built a tradition of simplicity and hard work that helped to shape the direction of the nation.

The New England Puritans had already behind them almost a century's experience of Protestant effort and thought. What was new, and of extreme importance, was the opportunity to carry these ideas into practice. This ideal was the dynamic motive that drove the Puritans across the Atlantic.

Even in New England, the Puritans were a small minority, when one considers effective church membership. But all the decisive movements in history are made by minorities, and the Puritans carried with them irresistible elements of strength. They knew exactly what they wanted; their polity was formulated and their discipline worked out.

The conception of a Bible commonwealth was clear to them. And to achieve the ends of this commonwealth, they had entered into a covenant with God and with one another. "We must be knit together in this work as one man, we must entertain each other in brotherly affection." They were embarked upon a mission: "We shall be as a city upon a hill, the eyes of

John Winthrop, 12 times governor of Massachusetts Bay, believed in a Bible commonwealth presided over by an elect minority.

all people are upon us." If they failed, God would make them "a story and a byword through the world, we shall open the mouths of enemies to speak evil of the ways of God and all professors for God's sake." If they succeeded, men would say of later settlements, "The Lord make it like that of New England." We recognize thus early the sense of mission that is so strong in the American make-up today. That came from the Bay Puritans, not from the Plymouth Pilgrims.

The cornerstone of all their churches was a covenant. We find it clearly stated by one of their mentors, the Elizabethan Henry Jacob, a generation before: "A free mutual consent of believers joining and covenanting to live as members of a holy society together in all religious and virtuous duties as Christ and his apostles did institute and practice."

It was this covenant that made them Congregationalists. The Pilgrims at Plymouth were rather a different case, though it seems to be questioned today whether they were absolutely Separatists, wishing to be regarded as utterly separated from the Church of England. They trace their ancestry to the Scrooby congregation, and its pastors and mentors, John Smyth, Richard Clyfton, John Robinson, Elder Brewster. As for the vastly more important Massachusetts Puritans, they held themselves to be Puritan congregations of the Church of England and regarded separation as a sin. They were out to set a better model, and by their example to convert the church at home.

As the *Talbot* drew away from Land's End in 1629—a part of the Puritans' first plantation fleet, the largest that had ever set sail for New England—Francis Higginson spoke these words to the passengers: "We will not say, as the Separatists were wont to say at their leaving of England, 'Farewell, Babylon! Farewell, Rome!' But we *will* say, 'Farewell, dear England! Farewell, the Church of God in England, and all the Christian friends there!' We do not go to New England as Separatists from the Church of England, though we cannot but separate from the corruptions in it, but we go to practice the positive part of Church Reformation, and propagate the Gospel in America."

The Pilgrims were self-effacing exiles who wanted only to escape attention in order to worship and live in their own way; the Massachusetts Puritans were a governing body going forth to convert others.

The 19th century immensely exaggerated the importance of the Pilgrim Fathers. Their story was told in countless books and then put into verse by Longfellow. To judge from its literature, anyone would think that America started with them. It *is* true that the Pilgrims had the advantage of priority, and thereby exerted an influence by the example they set of civil marriage and in the registering of deeds. Theirs also was the first Congregational church, a working model already in be-

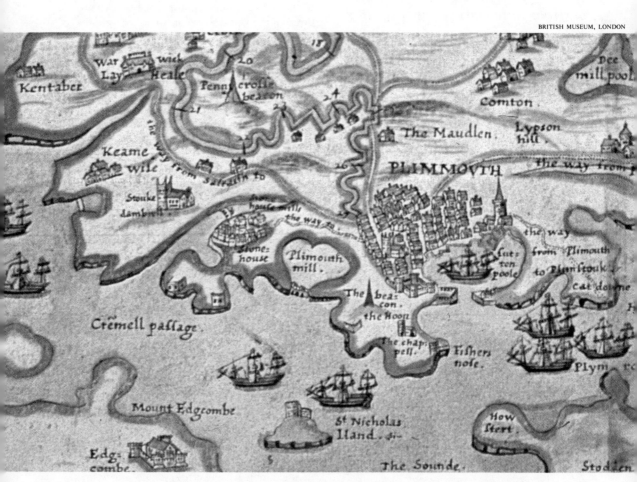

It was from Plymouth harbor, shown on this 1591 map with many surrounding towns, that the Pilgrims finally sailed on the Mayflower *for the New World on September 6, 1620.*

ing when the Massachusetts Puritans began to arrive. But in every other respect the influence was all the other way. The size, power, and importance of the Bay Colony began to tell, until ultimately it absorbed Plymouth.

The religion, and thereby the mentality, of New England was entirely English in its sources. The Scrooby flock had settled in Leyden, where John Robinson was publicly ordained as their pastor; William Brewster became their ruling elder. Prior to emigration, it was agreed that if a majority of the congregation volunteered, Robinson should go as their pastor. To his disappointment, only a minority volunteered. Only 37 of the 100 or more passengers on board the *Mayflower* were Pilgrims from Leyden; we do not know who the rest were, but some of them, we learn from William Bradford, were "profane fellows."

Robinson remained behind to minister to the majority. Meanwhile, he refused to sanction the administration of the sacraments by Elder Brewster in Plymouth. Not being ordained, Brewster might preach and pray, but not give communion. Robinson kept hoping he might be able to join them; he sent them spiritual advice, but soon he was dead. The state of the Pilgrims at Plymouth may be described as "Waiting for Robinson."

However, they got on well without him. Brewster, a mature man of 53 when they landed at Plymouth, had been at Peterhouse, Cambridge, where he acquired nonconforming ideas. He was postmaster in Scrooby, and a pillar of the congregation till 1608. The Scrooby flock left England because it was an ungodly land and found Amsterdam and, subsequently, Leyden uncongenial. Only the wilderness would do, and to the wilderness they went.

Social life in Plymouth has been described as "undoubtedly quiet in the extreme"; but Brewster, according to Bradford, was "of a very cheerful spirit, very sociable and pleasant amongst his friends." He had an excellent library—mostly theology, since he had to preach thrice a week. The rest was mainly practical—herbals, books of surveying and medicine, works on the culture of silkworms and varieties of timber. In addition were these worldly authors—Machiavelli's *Prince,* Bodin's *Republic,* Bacon's *Advancement of Learning,* and Raleigh's *Prerogatives of Parliaments in England.*

For company there was Miles Standish, Edward Winslow, and Governor Bradford, to whom Elder Brewster stood second in the little colony. Miles Standish was born about 1584, of a younger branch of an old Lancashire family. A professional soldier, he joined the Pilgrims as such, for in religion he was never one of them. He was given command of parties exploring the country and defending the colony against suspect Indians, on one occasion being responsible for a deed of blood against some Indian chiefs. In 1621, he was made captain of the colony, and was often an assistant to the governor. Next to Standish in dealing with the Indians was Winslow, also a man of good family who had joined the Leyden community. Above all, there was Governor Bradford. It is impossible to overestimate what the Plymouth Colony owed to him, for he was, like John Winthrop of the Bay Colony, ideally suited to govern. Bradford brought with him the same Elizabethan ideas on authority that Winthrop had: The main body of the people share in government "only in some weighty matters, when we think good." Queen Elizabeth might have subscribed to that.

As a youth affected by the preaching of Richard Clyfton, William Bradford joined the Scrooby flock and went with Robinson to Leyden. He disliked sectarian labels and wished to retain fellowship with all reformed churches, believing it "great arrogancy for any man or church to think that he or they have so sounded the word of God to the bottom." He was re-elected governor 30 times—almost continuously, in fact—in spite of the fear of the New England colonies of a governor for life, and it is obvious that the Pilgrims could not get on without him. His long rule was really one of a benevolent autocracy.

Though not a university man, Bradford was well read, and an excellent historian. His *History of Plymouth Plantation* is considered a masterpiece. In his well-stocked library he, too, had Bodin, Guicciardini's *History of*

Florence, and Peter Martyr's *Decades of the New World.* This Pilgrim governor, so wise, so sober, so restrained—an "achieved spirit," as his age would say—also owned a red waistcoat with silver buttons, a colored hat, and a violet cloak. But it is by his *History* that he lives. It has the qualities that give enduring life to a book—absolute fidelity, lifelikeness, and trustworthiness. Its moral purity—the selflessness, submission, and control—shines through.

For the Elizabethan background of Massachusetts we could not do better than look at the life lived in Groton in the years before John Winthrop left for America. In 1616, Winthrop began a record of his spiritual state, from which we gain an authentic picture of a Puritan's inner mind. John Winthrop felt he was not yet "resolved upon the denial of this world and myself." After his second wife's death he thought he "had brought under my rebellious flesh and prettily tamed it by moderate and spare diet and holding it somewhat close to its task, by prayer, reading, meditation, and the works of my calling." Nevertheless, when he tried to settle down to his ordinary tasks, he found that "the flesh had gotten head and heart again and began to linger after the world; the society of the saints seemed a contemptible thing, meditations were few, prayer was tedious, and fain would the flesh have been at an end before I began." Once more he put himself on a spare diet and set himself to reading devout books. After some time at this, he was surprised to find that he "grew very melancholic and uncomfortable," especially since he had refrained from any "outward conversation in the world." In this condition he began to enjoy experiences like those of St. John of the Cross and St. Theresa. He had such "a heavenly meditation of the love between Christ and me as ravished my heart with unspeakable joy; methought my soul had as familiar and sensible society with him as my wife could have with the kindest husband. I desired no other happiness but to be embraced of him." And, shortly, he was: "O my Lord, my love, how wholly delectable art thou! Let him kiss me with the kisses of his mouth, for his love is sweeter than wine; how

lovely is thy countenance! How pleasant are thy embracings!" This state of exaltation seems to have ended with his third marriage—and perhaps it was about time—in 1618, when his spiritual diary comes to an end. Winthrop got away from this morbid introspection; his impulses found normal channels of expression. He was able to turn to a legal career, becoming an attorney in the Court of Wards and a member of the Inner Temple. External considerations made him decide to go to America; the king's decision to dispense with Parliament meant there was no future for Puritans.

Those who met at Cambridge in August, 1629, and entered into an agreement to go included Thomas Dudley, Sir Richard Saltonstall, William Pynchon, Increase Nowell, and William Vassall. All were Elizabethans. Dudley, born at Northampton in 1576, was the son of a captain "slain in the wars." He enjoyed the ministrations of the Reverend John Cotton and kept in close touch with all the discussions preparatory to the move. He sailed on the *Arbella*—a more important ship than the *Mayflower,* for she carried Winthrop and the Massachusetts leadership on board. Although he was Winthrop's deputy governor, Dudley had a violent quarrel with him over the decision to move from their first site to Boston. They exchanged some ungodly, though not necessarily unpuritanical, words. The two men were hardly congenial. Dudley was dogmatic and overbearing; he had none of Winthrop's moderation, judgment, charm. A man of 54 when he landed in New England, Dudley was tough physically; he produced progeny at the age of 70. He was four times elected governor, 13 times deputy governor; he was one of the first overseers of Harvard, one of the two Massachusetts commissioners who formed the New England Confederation. He was something of a scholar and, like most Elizabethans, wrote verse. A last poem, found in his pocket after his death, spoke his mind on toleration:

Let men of God in courts and churches watch
O'er such as do a toleration hatch.

These lines were not without application to such as Saltonstall. Nephew to Sir Richard

The Pilgrims, shown walking to church, worshiped every Sunday from 8 to 12 in the morning and then would meet again in the late afternoon for another long service.

From left: John Cotton, the Bay Colony's great preacher; Richard Saltonstall, noble-man and Puritan; Josiah Winslow, founder of the first public school in Massachusetts.

Saltonstall, who had been lord mayor of London, he was one of the Puritan governing class who went over on the *Arbella*. But he did not see eye-to-eye with the rigid exclusiveness of the theocracy, and was twice fined for backsliding in regard to church matters. He returned home next year and never went back.

Pynchon, Nowell, Vassall—all three had trouble with the ruling authorities. Pynchon, who helped found Roxbury and Springfield, wrote a book in 1650 controverting the Calvinist view of the Atonement. When the General Court ordered the book burned, he "decided to return to England, where he might enjoy that liberty of opinion which was denied him in the colony he had helped to found."

In 1633, the two authoritative religious leaders of the first generation, John Cotton and Thomas Hooker, came over. They had been invited together, but it was wisely decided that "a couple of such great men might be more serviceable asunder than together." Samuel Stone accompanied them, so it was possible to say, in the punning manner of the time, that in Massachusetts they now had "Cotton for their clothing, Hooker for their fishing, and Stone for their building."

Cotton was probably the leading nonconforming clergyman in the Church of England, if it is not paradoxical to say so. He became

vicar of the English Boston, where he began to simplify the services in the interest of more preaching. He was a great preacher. He soon developed a faithful following. Like Winthrop, Cotton was a leader, and this was given full scope in Massachusetts, where, Roger Williams said, there were people who "could hardly believe that God would suffer Mr. Cotton to err."

Cotton and Winthrop were both Elizabethans in their point of view—men whose minds were geared to government. Cotton's chief works were in defense of the civil power's right to interfere in support of the truth, but he had no more illusions than Winthrop about the people's fitness to govern. "Democracy," he wrote, "I do not conceive that ever God did ordain as a fit government either for church or commonwealth." Nevertheless, there was in Protestantism an inner dynamic that led on to democracy, and this shortly became evident.

Thomas Hooker, the son of a Leicestershire yeoman, was a student at Queen's College, Cambridge, and became, like Cotton, a fellow of Emmanuel. At Esher, in Surrey, his patron's wife believed she had committed the unpardonable sin—whatever that was. Hooker succeeded in comforting her, where others failed. He had a way with him—to the soul. He married the lady's waiting woman—the proper social status for a clergyman's bride.

Hooker and Stone were called as pastor and teacher of Newton. But they and their congregation became restive under the self-sufficient autocracy of Massachusetts. Hooker's sermon at the making of the Connecticut constitution used to be thought a democratic declaration, for he stated that the "foundation of all authority is the free consent of the people." But we recognize in that the traditional social-contract doctrine as the base of society. "They who have the power to appoint officers and magistrates," he wrote, "it is in their power also to set the bounds and limitations of the power and place unto which they call them." We recognize in that the heart of American political conviction.

The bent of Hooker's mind was, however, evangelical. His books bear such titles as *The Soul's Preparation for Christ, The Soul's Vocation,* and *The Soul's Implantation.* From Con-

necticut, Hooker was called to take part in the controversies that raged in Massachusetts over the tiresome Roger Williams. No sooner had Williams landed in Massachusetts than he discovered that he was "once more in a land where the nonconforming were unfree." He responded by declaring that civil governments had no right to enforce religious injunctions, and when the civil authorities showed they had the power, he took refuge in Plymouth. Later, banished from Massachusetts, he founded a settlement in Providence, the beginning of Rhode Island. Imperial Massachusetts sought to invade Rhode Island and extinguish it; only an appeal to Old England secured a patent and freedom for it to exist.

The Puritans went out to set a model of a godly commonwealth for the world to see and follow. They suffered the fate of all who make an egoistic assumption as to the

On January 21, 1621, the Pilgrims came ashore and held their first religious services on American soil in the newly completed Common House, the first Plymouth building.

177

course history will take: The course it takes is never what they suppose. Nevertheless, the heroic effort, the sacrifice, had not been in vain. The legacy of the Elizabethan Puritans to New England, though different from what they expected, was a matter of the highest importance. It did not turn out to be New Jerusalem, but it turned out to provide the strongest of bonds to bind together a continental society of a new sort. Something strong, even astringent, was needed to hold together so vast a country; the New England mentality, when it lost the narrowness of its early beliefs, retained a distinguishing element—strongly ethical, seeing life in terms of obligation and duty rather than pleasure. Although the theology and the metaphysics had broken down, the Puritan character remained—the strongest factor in survival. In history, to survive is what matters.

The overwhelmingly theological complexion of the intellectual culture of New England reflected not so much Elizabethan England as Elizabethan Puritanism. But we must not underrate its intellectual energy. Samuel Eliot Morison tells us that "the dominant Puritan clergy, far from being indifferent to culture, did everything possible to stimulate, promote, and even produce intellectual activity. Moreover, it was largely the clergy who persuaded a poor and struggling people to set up schools and a college which continued to serve the community in later centuries."

Their handicaps in keeping civilized standards going were tremendous; theirs was a pioneer country strenuously engaged in the struggle for existence. Yet within 10 years of its founding, Massachusetts had a vigorous intellectual life of its own. No other English commonwealth attempted to provide for learning so soon after it was founded. But New England had Elizabethan England behind it, with its enthusiasm for education, fortified by the Puritan belief in intellect. New Englanders proved their beliefs not only in their precepts but in their works: They were ready to tax themselves for things that in Old England were provided by endowment.

These were the things of the mind, and their minds were formed by the English universities, especially by Cambridge, from which most of the leaders came. There was an average of one university man to every 40 or 50 families— much higher than in Old England. Morison tells us that Puritanism "preserved far more of the humanist tradition than did non-Puritanism in other English colonies." It devoted more attention to classical scholarship and therefore had an interest in making verses, such as all English students were taught to write. So, too, with literary form and style. Morison points out that "the older founders of New England grew up in the age of Shakespeare and the King James Bible," and in consequence these men "wrote prose superior by any standard to that of the later, native-born writers."

However, Shakespeare was precisely what the New England Puritans excluded. They would have suppressed the Elizabethan drama if they could. They had no appreciation of the majesty of the Roman Catholic Church, the Rome of Sixtus V, the music of Palestrina. They had nothing but dislike for the grave and ordered beauty of the Anglican Church, the cadences of the Book of Common Prayer.

The Puritan attitude involved in some ways a denial of life. It was antagonistic to the glorification of the natural man, with all his instincts and appetites, that characterized the Renaissance and the great Elizabethans.

On the other hand, some contraction of response, some repression, produces greater strength and energy with which to face the harsh, sad conditions of pioneer life. And for the life of their community, in probity and public spirit, in moral responsibility and uprightness, in humaneness as to punishment and in mutual help in need, in simple godliness—whether we believe or no, regarding it as a human fact—they *did* exemplify higher standards than any other English society. And theirs more than any others' was the making of the nation.

A. L. Rowse, a fellow of All Souls College, Oxford, and the British Academy, was the author of The Elizabethans in America, The England of Elizabeth, *and many other books.*

Volume 2
ENCYCLOPEDIC SECTION

The two-page reference guide below lists the entries by categories. The entries in this section supplement the subject matter covered in the text of this volume. A **cross-reference** (*see*) means that a separate entry appears elsewhere in this section. However, certain important persons and events mentioned here have individual entries in the Encyclopedic Section of another volume. Consult the Index in Volume 18.

COLONIAL GOVERNORS

Sir Edmund Andros (New England)
Sir William Berkeley (Virginia)
Sir Francis Bernard (Massachusetts)
William Bradford (Plymouth)
Charles Calvert (Maryland)
Leonard Calvert (Maryland)
Robert Dinwiddie (Virginia)
Joseph Dudley (Massachusetts)
Thomas Dudley (Massachusetts)
Theophilus Eaton (New Haven)

John Endecott (Massachusetts)
Count Louis de Frontenac (New France)
Thomas Hutchinson (Massachusetts)
Thomas Morton (Merry Mount)
Increase Nowell (Massachusetts)
James Oglethorpe (Georgia)
William Penn (Pennsylvania)
Sir Henry Vane (Massachusetts)
Roger Williams (Rhode Island)
Edward Winslow (Plymouth)
John Winthrop (Massachusetts)

COLONIAL POLITICS

Samuel Adams
Albany Plan of Union
Crispus Attucks
Bacon's Rebellion
Boston Massacre
Boston Tea Party
Committees of Correspondence
Connecticut Charter of 1662
Gaspee
Patrick Henry

House of Burgesses
Massacre of 1770
Navigation Acts
James Otis
Sons of Liberty
Stamp Act
Sugar Act
Townshend Acts
Triangular trade
Virginia Resolves
Abraham Whipple

COLONIAL PROPRIETORS

John Berkeley (Carolina, New Jersey)
Sir William Berkeley (Carolina)
Charles Calvert (Maryland)
George Calvert (Maryland)

Leonard Calvert (Maryland)
Carolina Proprietors
Sir George Carteret (Carolina, New Jersey)
William Penn (Pennsylvania)
Thomas Weston (Plymouth)

COLONIAL THOUGHT AND CULTURE

James Adair

John Bartram

Anne Bradstreet

Stephen Day

John Harvard

John Locke

Cotton Mather

Thomas Morton

Mary Rowlandson

Edward Taylor

Michael Wigglesworth

John Peter Zenger

EUROPEAN LEADERS

Charles I (England)

Charles II (England)

Oliver Cromwell (England)

Frederick II (Prussia)

George II (England)

George Grenville (England)

James II (England)

Louis XIV (France)

William Pitt (England)

EXPLORERS

James Adair

Jean Allouez

Juan Bautista de Anza

Vitus Bering

Hudson's Bay Company

Louis Jolliet

Robert Cavelier de La Salle

Jacques Marquette

INDIAN WARS

Acadia

Albany Plan of Union

Jeffrey Amherst

War of the Austrian Succession

Edward Braddock

Deerfield Massacre

Fort Duquesne

French and Indian War

Iroquois League

War of Jenkins' Ear

King George's War

King Philip's War

King William's War

Marquis Louis Joseph de Montcalm

Peace of Ryswick

Pequots

Pontiac

Queen Anne's War

War of the Spanish Succession

Treaty of Aix-La-Chapelle

Treaty of Utrecht

Tuscarora War

James Wolfe

PILGRIMS

John Alden

William Bradford

William Brewster

Miles Standish

PURITANS

Arbella

John Cotton

John Davenport

Francis Higginson

Thomas Hooker

Massachusetts Bay Company

Cotton Mather

Increase Mather

Richard Mather

New England Company

New Haven Colony

Richard Saltonstall

Samuel Sewall

Samuel Stone

William Vassall

John White

RELIGION

Congregationalism

Jonathan Edwards

John Eliot

Great Awakening

Half-Way Covenant

Anne Hutchinson

William Pynchon

Quakers

Salem witchcraft trials

Roger Williams

A

ACADIA. Probably of Indian origin, Acadia was the name of territories settled by the French from 1632 to 1713. It lay between the St. Lawrence River and the Atlantic and included Nova Scotia, New Brunswick, and the eastern part of Maine. Acadia was the scene of fighting during the colonial wars between Britain and France and was eventually ceded to England by the **Treaty of Utrecht** (*see*) in 1713. However, by 1755 colonial warfare had again erupted between the two powers (*see* **French and Indian War**). The English regarded the French settlers as an internal security risk and charged them with disloyalty. The Acadians were forced to leave their homes and were taken south to other English colonies. The severity of their hardships was described in 1847 by Henry Wadsworth Longfellow in his poem *Evangeline*. Some of the Acadians eventually settled in Louisiana, where their descendants are known today as Cajuns. A number of others later returned to Nova Scotia.

British ships carried off the French Acadians, whose homes were burned.

ADAIR, James (1709?–1783?). Adair was an Irish-born pioneer who traded with, fought for, and lived among the Indian tribes of South Carolina for 33 years (1735–1768). During that time, he kept a careful record of his experiences. His observations were published in London in 1775 under the title *The History of the American Indians*. Adair's book, which contains detailed accounts of the customs, languages, and rituals of such Indian tribes as the Cherokees and Chickasaws, has remained an important source of information about the American Indian. Adair is believed to have died in North Carolina after the Revolution.

ADAMS, Samuel (1722–1803). Samuel Adams was a leading agitator and propagandist for American independence from Great Britain. He was born in Boston and graduated from Harvard in 1740. Adams was unsuccessful as a businessman. However, he gained a great deal of influence because of his activities in various political clubs in Boston, and he played a major role in almost every confrontation between England and the Massachu-

setts Bay Colony in the years preceding the Revolution. As a member (1765–1774) of the Massachusetts legislature, Adams became an outspoken critic of British military and customs officials. He helped to organize the **Sons of Liberty** (*see*) in 1765. He was also involved in the events surrounding the **Boston Massacre** (*see*) in 1770, after which he forced the acting governor, **Thomas Hutchinson** (*see*), to withdraw British troops from the city. In addition, Adams helped to organize opposition to the **Sugar Act,** the **Stamp Act,** and the **Townshend Acts** (*see all*). In 1772, Adams started the Massachusetts **Committees of Correspondence** (*see*). In 1773, he helped to plan the **Boston Tea Party** (*see*). As a delegate to the First Continental Congress in 1774, Adams urged a complete breakaway from England. He subsequently was a signer of the Declaration of Independence. Adams later served as lieutenant governor (1789–1793) and governor (1794–1797) of Massachusetts. He died in Boston on October 2, 1803.

ALBANY PLAN OF UNION. Drafted by Benjamin Franklin (1706–1790), the Albany Plan sought to unify English colonies in America under a central administration for mutual defense. In the summer of 1754, shortly before the **French and Indian War** (*see*) broke out, representatives from Massachusetts, Rhode Island, Connecticut, New York, New Hampshire, Pennsylvania, and Maryland met at Albany, New York, with chieftains of the Six Nations (*see* **Iroquois League**). Their prime objective was to consolidate Indian support against the French. This aim was realized only in part, because the Iroquois were angry over colonial intrusions on their lands. The colonists then considered Franklin's proposal to form a loose confederation of colonies under a central government. The Albany Plan called for a federal union administered by a president general (appointed by the king) and a council of delegates from the colonies. Each colony would retain its separate existence, but the new government would have broad powers over taxation, Indian affairs, conscription, forts, and vessels. The Albany Plan met with unanimous approval by the delegates, but it was rejected by the crown, which feared that the union would endanger English influence in America. It was also turned down by the colonial legislatures, which believed it would lessen their independence. Despite its rejection, the Albany Plan was an important forerunner of later attempts at unification.

ALDEN, John (1599?–1687). Alden, a cooper, was hired by the Pilgrims at Southampton to repair the barrels aboard the *Mayflower* on its voyage to America in 1620. He was one of the signers of the Mayflower Compact and was one of the eight men who assumed responsibility for the colonial debt in 1627. Shortly after the landing at Plymouth, Alden married Priscilla Mullens, the daughter of a Pilgrim. The supposed involvement of his friend **Miles Standish** (*see*) in their courtship was popularized in 1858 by Henry Wadsworth Longfellow in his poem *The Courtship of Miles Standish*. Alden became a farmer in Duxbury, near Plymouth, and held a number of official positions in the colony. He was twice the governor's assistant (1633–1641 and 1650–1686) and frequently served as acting governor. Alden outlived all

John and Priscilla Alden

the other signers of the Mayflower Compact. When he died in 1687, he was buried close to Standish in Duxbury.

ALLOUEZ, Claude Jean (1622–1689). In 1658, Allouez, a Jesuit priest, sailed from France to Canada to help convert the Indian tribes of the Great Lakes region to Christianity. Over the next 31 years, Allouez baptized more than 10,000 Indians and purportedly preached to 100,000 Indians. He founded numerous missions, including those in the Wisconsin communities of Green Bay, Oshkosh, and De Pere. Allouez spent the last 12 years of his life among the Illinois Indians, carrying on the missionary work begun by **Jacques Marquette** (*see*). He died on August 27, 1689, while living among the Miamis in Michigan.

AMHERST, Jeffrey (1717–1797). A British career officer, Amherst was put in command of an expedition to North America in 1758 during the **French and Indian War** (*see*). He captured Louisbourg that same year, Ticonderoga in 1759, and Montreal in 1760. As a reward for his service, Amherst was made governor-general of England's enlarged holdings in North America. He held the post for three years (1760–1763) before returning to England, where he was made a baron in 1776. He died on August 31, 1797. Amherst College in Massachusetts, founded in 1821, is named for him.

ANDROS, Sir Edmund (1637–1714). Andros was an unpopular British administrator whose tyrannical rule of New England prompted colonists to revolt against him in 1689. Three years earlier he had been named governor of the Dominion of New England, which included Massachusetts, Rhode Island, Connecticut, Plymouth, and New Hampshire. New York and New Jersey were added to his jurisdiction in 1688. The consolidation was intended to bolster British defenses against the French. As governor, Andros sought to alter existing colonial charters (*see* **Connecticut Charter of 1662**). Aroused by his interference, colonists in Boston, at the urging of **Cotton Mather** (*see*), deposed and imprisoned Andros on April 18, 1689. He was sent back to England, but no charges were pressed against him. Andros later served as governor of Virginia (1692–1697) and briefly as governor of Maryland (1693–1694). He returned to England in 1697 and died in London.

ANZA, Juan Bautista de (1735–1788?). The Presidio (fortified settlement) of San Francisco was founded in 1776 by Juan de Anza, a Spanish adventurer who was one of the first to explore overland routes from New Mexico to California. During the early 1770s, Spain sent a number of expeditions north along the California coast. The Spaniards wanted to settle the area before the English and the Russians arrived. By 1771, they had established missions at Monterey and Los Angeles. Anza was put in command of an expedition—composed of 240 soldiers, settlers, and servants—which set out from the Presidio of Tubac in 1775. His orders were to colonize the San Francisco Bay region. He chose the site where San Francisco was formally founded on September 17, 1776. A year later, Anza was appointed governor of New Mexico, an area that included the present states of Arizona and New Mexico and parts of Nevada, Utah, Texas, Colorado, and California. Deposed in 1788, he vanished from the recorded history of the period.

ARBELLA. Until the *Arbella*'s arrival at Plymouth on June 12, 1630—10 years after the *Mayflower*—the colony had neither a charter nor a governor. The *Arbella* was the flagship of a small fleet that carried nearly 700 colonists, the largest group up to that time to immigrate to the New World. Aboard the *Arbella* was **John Winthrop** (*see*), who had been elected the first governor of the Massachusetts Bay Colony. He and other members of the recently formed **Massachusetts Bay Company** (*see*) had with them a charter that empowered them to establish the Commonwealth of Massachusetts.

ATTUCKS, Crispus (1723?–1770). Little is known about the early life of Attucks, who was one of the five colonials killed in the **Boston** Massacre (*see*). He was probably a sailor of black and Indian ancestry. On the night of March 5, 1770, Attucks was at the head of a crowd of waterfront rowdies that marched from the docks to the Old State House (*see pp. 140–141*). A mob had already formed in front of the building and was throwing snowballs and shouting angry taunts at a lone sentry. A group of soldiers ran out of their nearby barracks to aid the sentry. According to witnesses, Attucks "had heartiness enough to fall in upon them [the soldiers] and with one hand took hold of the bayonet and with the other knocked the man down." The British fired into the mob, shooting five persons, Attucks among them. His body was put on view at the Boston meeting hall and then buried in a common grave with the other victims. The incident was used as propaganda against the British by such firebrands as **Samuel Adams** (*see*). His cousin John Adams (1735–1826), the future second President, defended the British soldiers accused of the slayings. In court, Adams argued that Attucks had organized and led the mob. He described Attucks as a stout man "whose very look was enough to

Crispus Attucks' initials appear on this 1770 broadside published in Boston.

terrify any person. . . ." Of the nine soldiers put on trial, only two were convicted. They were branded on the hand as punishment. Although the sentences were intended to calm the citizens of Boston, colonial propagandists made martyrs of the victims (*see p. 160*).

AUSTRIAN SUCCESSION, War of the. *See* **King George's War.**

B

BACON'S REBELLION. In 1676, Nathaniel Bacon, Jr. (1647–1676), a wealthy planter, led an armed revolt against the governor of Virginia, **Sir William Berkeley** (*see*). Although historians disagree on the exact cause of the rebellion, they generally ascribe it to discontent over the strict enforcement of the **Navigation Acts** (*see*), the harshness of Berkeley's regime, and Berkeley's failure to provide protection from Indian attacks. Bacon used the slaying of his overseer by Indians as an excuse for starting the rebellion. In May, 1676, he led a group of planters to the southern frontier of Virginia and massacred a friendly Indian tribe. When Berkeley attempted to stop Bacon, Bacon marched to Jamestown in June and there forced the Virginia legislators to give him their consent to fight the Indians. Berkeley's efforts to oppose Bacon brought about civil war. Bacon drove Berkeley to the east coast of Virginia, and then, after a new legislature under rebel control was elected, Bacon burned Jamestown so that it would not fall into Berkeley's hands. Bacon was preparing to enact tax and voting reforms when he suddenly developed a fever and died on October 18,

1676. The rebellion evaporated. By February, 1677, Berkeley had reestablished his authority and ordered a number of Bacon's followers executed.

BARTRAM, John (1699–1777). Bartram, a self-taught American botanist, maintained a garden near Philadelphia and experimented in raising hybrid plants. The garden was a favorite resort of many colonial leaders, including George Washington and Benjamin Franklin. It is now a part of Philadelphia's park system and still contains trees planted by Bartram. One contemporary called him the greatest "natural botanist" of his time.

BERING, Vitus (1681–1741). This Danish sea captain was hired by Russia to explore Siberia. In the course of this exploration, he discovered Alaska in 1741. He made two voyages for the Russians. On the first, in 1728, he sailed through the strait—later named Bering Strait—that separates Siberia from Alaska, but sighted no land. On his second voyage 13 years later, Bering personally sighted the St. Elias Mountains on July 16, 1741. A landing party subsequently explored part of the Alaska coast. During a storm, Bering's ship, the *St. Peter,* was driven ashore and wrecked on the beach of the island now named for him. He died there on December 8, 1741. Months later, the survivors of his crew, ill from scurvy, finally reached the coast of the Kamchatka Peninsula and safety.

BERKELEY, John (?–1678). Together with his younger brother, **Sir William Berkeley,** and **Sir George Carteret** (*see both*), Lord Berkeley was one of eight so-called **Carolina Proprietors** (*see*) who received grants of land in the Carolinas during the early 1660s from **Charles II** (*see*). All had been supporters of the monarchy during the English Civil War. John Berkeley and Carteret were also granted joint proprietorship of New Jersey in 1664. Berkeley sold his New Jersey rights 10 years later to two Quaker friends of **William Penn** (*see*).

BERKELEY, Sir William (1606– 1677). William Berkeley, a younger brother of **John Berkeley** (*see*), was appointed governor of Virginia in 1641 by **Charles I** (*see*) of England. Initially, he was successful as an administrator and was popular with the colonists. He encouraged and developed farming, conducted useful agricultural experiments on his own estates, and promoted practical crafts, such as weaving and the home production of cloth. His defeat of the Indians ensured peace for many years. When a Dutch fleet tried to invade Virginia in 1665, his well-organized defense prevented the Dutch from landing. During the English Civil War, Berkeley offered sanctuary in Vir-

COURTESY OF MR. M. DU PONT LEE

Sir William Berkeley

ginia to the future **Charles II** (*see*). He encouraged royalists to settle there and refused to acknowledge the government of **Oliver Cromwell** (*see*). He was eventually forced to surrender in 1652 when threatened by an English fleet offshore. Berkeley retired to his plantations and lived quietly until the Restoration of Charles II in 1660, when he was reinstated as governor by the colonists. Although he protested to London against the inequities of the **Navigation Acts** (*see*), his rule of the colony became increasingly autocratic and violent. Berkeley's religious intolerance, his hatred of Puritans and **Quakers** (*see*), and his tyrannical rule culminated in **Bacon's Rebellion** (*see*) in 1676. His cruel punishment of the rebels, many of whom were executed, led to his recall the following year by Charles, who reportedly said, "The old fool has put to death more people in that naked country than I did here for the murder of my father [Charles I]." Berkeley died in England on July 9, 1677.

BERNARD, Sir Francis (1712– 1779). Bernard's nine years as governor of Massachusetts (1760– 1769) were turbulent ones. The **Sugar Act,** the **Stamp Act** (*see both*), and the quartering of troops at Boston were all bitterly contested during his term of office. Bernard had been born into an influential English family. He practiced law before coming to the colonies in 1758 as governor of New Jersey. Transferred to Massachusetts in 1760, he incurred the angry opposition of the colonists by trying to enforce the repressive English laws. Although Bernard was sympathetic to demands that certain tax levies be lowered or abolished, he failed to understand the intensity of the colonists' po-

Sir Francis Bernard

litical discontent. In his reports to England, he misrepresented conditions in America. Some of his letters to officials in London fell into colonial hands and were published in 1769. As a result, the Massachusetts Assembly demanded his removal from office. Bernard returned to England that same year. He died there on June 16, 1779.

BOSTON MASSACRE. Before the Revolution, the Boston Massacre was the most violent outbreak of colonial hostility to British rule in America. Its result —the death of five men—was widely publicized throughout the colonies and further increased resentment of the British. The incident, which took place on March 5, 1770, began with a fistfight between a Boston worker and a British soldier. Afterward, restless crowds of citizens and troops of soldiers roamed the streets. About nine o'clock that night, a group of rowdies harassed a sentry outside the Old State House. Captain Thomas Preston (1730–?) and a squad of

soldiers came to the sentry's aid. Without orders, some of his troops fired into the angry crowd. Three men, including **Crispus Attucks** (*see*), were killed and two were mortally wounded. A full-scale uprising was averted when **Samuel Adams** (*see*) demanded that the acting governor, **Thomas Hutchinson** (*see*), withdraw all British troops in Boston to islands in the harbor. Hutchinson, anxious to avoid further bloodshed, complied. Preston and eight of his men were subsequently charged with murder and tried in Boston. Preston and six soldiers were acquitted. Two soldiers were found guilty of manslaughter. They were branded on the hand and released. Paul Revere (1735–1818) made an engraving of the incident (*see p. 160*) that was used as propaganda by American patriots to build up anti-British sentiment.

BOSTON TEA PARTY. The immediate cause of the Boston Tea Party in 1773 was the attempt of the East India Company, a British trading monopoly, to bring cut-rate tea into the American colonies. The colonists, already

angered by British trade restrictions, were afraid that the shipments would hurt domestic tea traders and lead to an English monopoly of the American market. They asked the governor, **Thomas Hutchinson** (*see*), to order all English vessels loaded with tea back to England, but he refused. On the night of December 16, the **Sons of Liberty** (*see*) disguised themselves as Mohawk Indians. They boarded the merchant ships in the harbor and dumped 342 chests of tea into the bay. The English retaliated by revoking the Massachusetts Bay Colony's charter and closing the Port of Boston. In addition, Parliament also enacted laws to protect British officials in quelling riots, broadened the rules governing the quartering of troops in colonial homes, and realigned Canada's boundary to the detriment of the American colonies.

BRADDOCK, Edward (1695– 1755). After 43 years of service in England's elite Coldstream Guards, Braddock was promoted in 1754 to major general and given command of all British

Cheered by colonists, "Indians" dump British tea into Boston Harbor.

Edward Braddock

forces in North America. His military powers were the broadest ever granted a colonial commander in chief. His orders were to capture **Fort Duquesne** (*see*), a key French stronghold in western Pennsylvania, on the site of present-day Pittsburgh. Braddock's army, composed of about 700 colonials and 1,400 British regulars, had to cut a road over the Allegheny Mountains in order to reach the French outpost. Progress was very slow. While still 80 miles from his objective, Braddock decided to take the advice of his aide, Colonel George Washington, and drop his heavy transport. One-third of Braddock's troops remained behind with the supply wagons. On July 9, 1755, eight miles from Fort Duquesne, a combined force of 900 French and Indians, firing from concealed positions, ambushed the English army (*see pp. 110–113*). Braddock refused to order his troops to protect themselves behind trees. After three hours of fighting, half of the English army was either dead or wounded. Braddock himself had four horses shot out from under him during the clash and was wounded. He died four days later. The road his army cleared later became a major highway used by pioneers heading west.

BRADFORD, William (1590?– 1657). The early prosperity of the Pilgrims at Plymouth was due primarily to the leadership of Bradford, its second governor. Bradford had joined the Separatists at Scrooby, England, in 1606 and had migrated with the congregation to Holland in 1609. He sailed aboard the *Mayflower* and was a signer of the Mayflower Compact on November 11, 1620. In his *History of Plimmoth Plantation,* written between 1630 and 1651, Bradford described the departure of the Separatists from Holland and coined the term *Pilgrim,* "They knew they were pilgrimes, & looked not much on those things, but lifted up their eyes to ye heavens, their dearest country, and quieted their spirits." Upon the death of the colony's first governor, John Carver (1576?– 1621), Bradford was elected in April, 1621, to the first of 30 year-long terms in office. His rule was that of a benevolent autocrat— firm but judicious. Through the first difficult years, he helped save the colony from starvation and kept peace with the Indians and among the settlers. Bradford and seven other Pilgrims purchased control of the colony in 1627 from merchant investors in London. He kept a monopoly on Plymouth's trade and fishing to pay his huge personal debt, but he distributed the land and cattle equally among the other settlers.

BRADSTREET, Anne (1612?– 1672). America's first lady of letters wrote two collections of poetry and formed the first literary circle in the Massachusetts Bay Colony. Anne was a member of the group led by **John Winthrop** (*see*), which sailed to New England on the *Arbella* (*see*) in 1630. She was accompanied by her husband, Simon Bradstreet (1603– 1697), and her father, **Thomas Dudley** (*see*), both of whom were to hold important administrative positions in the colony, including the governorship. The Bradstreets settled at Ipswich, and in about 1644 they moved to North Andover. Anne found time between her duties in raising eight children to compose poetry. Without telling Anne, a relative had a book of her poems, *The Tenth Muse Lately Sprung Up in America,* published in England in 1650. The verses are moralistic and religious in content, and they reflect a typically Puritan viewpoint. A second anthology, published in 1678, after her death, contains fewer theological musings and more simple scenes from the New England world as Anne saw it.

BREWSTER, William (1566?– 1644). Although he was not an ordained minister, Brewster was largely responsible for establishing the Pilgrim church at Plymouth Colony. Exposed to nonconformist ideas while studying (1580–1582) at Cambridge University in England, Brewster believed that Christianity should be returned to a "primative order, libertie & bewtie." He formally broke with the Church of England in 1606 and worshiped with the Separatists at the village of Scrooby (*see pp. 54–55*). In 1608, he accompanied the group to Holland, where he printed Separatist pamphlets for distribution in England. As a ruling elder of the Pilgrim church, Brewster helped secure permission for the Pilgrims to immigrate to America. He left on the *Mayflower* in 1620. Brewster conducted church services for the colony until the arrival of a parson in 1629. He also assisted in the administration of Plymouth's affairs and, along with **William Bradford** (*see*), was a key figure in the colony's survival. He died on April 10, 1644.

C

CALVERT, Charles (1637–1715). Charles Calvert was installed as governor of Maryland in 1661 by his father, Cecilius Calvert (1605–1675). He became the proprietor of the colony on his father's death. By this time, Protestants in the colony far outnumbered Roman Catholics, most of whom had been encouraged to settle in Maryland by the Calverts. In 1676, the Protestants rebelled against Calvert's autocratic rule but were soon suppressed. In 1684, Calvert returned to England to defend the colony's charter in a dispute with **William Penn** (*see*) about the Maryland-Pennsylvania boundary. His defense succeeded, but the colonial government in Maryland was over-

Charles Calvert

thrown by Protestants during his absence. A royal government was proclaimed in 1692, and Calvert never returned. Also known as the Third Lord Baltimore, Calvert continued to argue for his territorial rights in Maryland until his death in 1715.

CALVERT, George (1580?–1632). Calvert, an Englishman interested in colonizing North America, founded Maryland in 1632 as a refuge for Roman Catholics. He was a staunch supporter of James I (1566–1625) in Parliament but resigned in 1625 after he converted to Catholicism. The king then made him Baron Baltimore of Baltimore, Ireland, and granted him large Irish estates. Calvert decided to found a new colony overseas to enable Catholics to worship without fear of persecution. In 1621, he established a settlement called Avalon in New Foundland. He visited it in 1627 but found the climate too harsh. Calvert petitioned **Charles I** (*see*) for land farther south. In 1632, he received a tract of land that he named Maryland after the queen, Henrietta Maria (1609–1669). The territory included land regarded by Virginians as part of their colony. Calvert, who is also called the First Lord Baltimore, died shortly before his charter was confirmed. The grant passed to his eldest son, Cecilius Calvert (1605–1675), who never visited Maryland but delegated his authority to his brother, **Leonard Calvert** (*see*).

CALVERT, Leonard (1606–1647). Leonard Calvert was the second son of **George Calvert** (*see*) and the younger brother of Cecilius Calvert (1605–1675). He went to Maryland in 1634 to represent his brother, who held the colony's charter. The Calverts were Roman

Catholics who hoped to make Maryland a refuge for Catholic worshipers. In 1637, Leonard Calvert was commissioned as governor, chief magistrate, and commander in chief of all land and naval forces in the colony. He maintained peaceful trading relations with the Indians but ran into trouble with the existing Protestant majority in the colony. Calvert agreed to govern according to the laws of England, but in 1644 a Protestant uprising forced him to flee to Virginia. He returned in 1646 with an army of colonists from Maryland and Virginia and reestablished his authority. The following year he died.

CAROLINA PROPRIETORS. The Carolina Proprietors were eight English royalists who were given territory in North America in 1663 as a reward for their loyalty to the crown during the English Civil War. Among the proprietors were **John Berkeley, Sir William Berkeley,** and **Sir George Carteret** (*see all*). The lands, granted by **Charles II** (*see*), extended along the Atlantic coast from about Albemarle Sound in present-day North Carolina to approximately the southern border of present-day Georgia. The grants extended westward to the "south seas" (the Pacific). The proprietors attracted settlers to the territory by promising them land, religious freedom, and limited self-government. However, when it became clear that the grants were not returning any profits, the proprietors lost interest in the settlements, and in 1719 the colonists revolted. England took over South Carolina as a crown colony the same year and purchased North Carolina as a crown colony 10 years later.

CARTERET, Sir George (1610?–1680). Carteret was an English royalist whose defense of the Channel island of Jersey against the Puritan forces of **Oliver Cromwell** (*see*) led to his being awarded grants of land in the Carolinas. He was one of eight so-called **Carolina Proprietors** (*see*) given lands in the American colony in 1660 following the Restoration of **Charles II** (*see*). In 1664, the Duke of York, later **James II** (*see*), turned over some of his own grants to Carteret and **John Berkeley** (*see*). These lands, which lay between the Hudson and Delaware Rivers, were named New Jersey in Carteret's honor. After his death, Carteret's widow sold her holdings in New Jersey to **William Penn** and other **Quakers** (*see both*).

CHARLES I (1600–1649). This English monarch's support of the Church of England and its persecution of religious minorities prompted a great migration of Puritans to America (*see pp. 95–96*) during his reign (1625–1649). Because Charles was constantly arguing with Parliament over religious and political rights, he neglected the administration of the American colonies. Charles refused to share his authority with Parliament, which wanted the power to approve tax policies and judicial appointments. In 1629, he dismissed Parliament and ruled for 11 years without calling another one. He was forced to recall Parliament in 1640 in order to raise funds. This Parliament, known as the Short Parliament, demanded that he assure religious freedom in England. Charles immediately dismissed it, too. Another Parliament, known as the Long Parliament, was convened the same year. It informed Charles that he would need its consent to dissolve it. Charles promised to end religious persecutions and not to levy new taxes without Parliament's approval. However, he failed to keep both promises, and after he tried to arrest five members of Parliament, the English Civil War broke out in 1642. The king's opponents, led by **Oliver Cromwell** (*see*), defeated the royal forces in 1645. Charles himself fell into the hands of Parliament in 1647. He was tried for treason and beheaded on January 30, 1649. Charles' death marked the end of absolute monarchy in England.

CHARLES II (1630–1685). The reign (1660–1685) of Charles II was a period of significant advance in the colonization of America. The son of **Charles I** (*see*), he ascended the English throne in 1660 at the time of the Restoration. Known as the Merry Monarch, Charles was more interested in athletics, the arts, and social activities than governmental affairs. In 1664, Charles granted his brother, the Duke of York, later **James II** (*see*), the former Dutch colony of New Netherland. The duke, in turn, gave the present area of New Jersey to **George Carteret** and **John Berkeley** (*see both*). **William Penn** (*see*) received what is now Pennsylvania from Charles in 1681 in payment for a debt owed to Penn's father (*see pp. 103–105*). Charles suffered a stroke and died in 1685.

COMMITTEES OF CORRESPONDENCE. In order to spread anti-British propaganda and organize the colonists, **Samuel Adams** (*see*) formed the first Committee of Correspondence in Boston in November, 1772. Three months later it was estimated that there were more than 80 committees in Massachusetts alone. Similar committees were started throughout the colonies in the next two years. These were formed on the county level and were responsible to an intercolonial Committee of Cor-

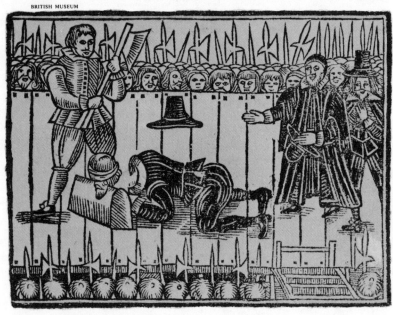

Londoners reportedly groaned in despair when Charles I was beheaded.

respondence formed in 1773 by Thomas Jefferson (1743–1826), **Patrick Henry** (*see*), and Richard Henry Lee (1732–1794). Besides directing public opinion in their area, some of these county groups enacted and enforced laws and set up courts to settle disputes. Although called Committees of Correspondence, the groups organized by Virginia in March, 1773, were in reality standing committees of that colony's legislature.

CONGREGATIONALISM. *See* **Half-Way Covenant.**

CONNECTICUT CHARTER OF 1662. The colonists of Conncecticut governed themselves from 1635 under a patent for settlement. However, they worried that this patent did not insure the ownership of land in the colony. When **Charles II** (*see*) became king following the Restoration in 1660, they decided to seek a formal charter. In 1661, they sent John Winthrop (1606–1676), the son of the Massachusetts Bay Colony's first governor, **John Winthrop** (*see*), to England to petition the king. The charter he received, dated April 23, 1662, was so liberal that it virtually granted complete freedom. Its jurisdiction included the New Haven Colony, which joined the Connecticut Colony in January, 1665. The charter was the law of the colony until 1685, when **James II** (*see*) became king. James tried to annul many existing charters, including Connecticut's. Although the colonists sought to keep their charter, **Sir Edmund Andros** (*see*), governor of the newly created Dominion of New England, was sent to take control of Connecticut. He arrived in Hartford with an armed troop on October 31, 1687. The next day, Andros publicly read his orders annexing the colony to the dominion, and according to tradition, demanded possession of the charter, which was brought in. However, while the colony's governor, Robert Treat (1622?–1710), was speaking heatedly against its surrender, the lamps suddenly went out and the charter disappeared. It was seized by a colonist who hid it in a hollow tree. Despite the loss of the charter, Andros governed the colonists for the next two years, until the overthrow of James II. Legal experts in England subsequently ruled that the charter had never been voided and was still in effect. Amended after the Revolution, the charter served as the basic law of Connecticut until 1818. The tree where it had been secreted became known as the Charter Oak and remained a patriotic landmark until it fell in 1856.

COTTON, John (1584–1652). Sometimes called the Patriarch of New England, Cotton played a major role in the development of the Congregational Church in the Massachusetts Bay Colony (*see* **Massachusetts Bay Company**). In 1612, Cotton, then an Anglican minister, was chosen vicar of St. Botolph's Church in Boston, England, but he eventually abandoned the ceremonies of the Church of England in favor of the simpler Puritan forms of worship. As a result, he was forced to resign in 1632. Cotton decided to join his friend **John Winthrop** (*see*) in America. The capital of the Massachusetts Bay Colony was named Boston in honor of Cotton's former parish. Cotton was the teacher in the First Church of Boston from 1633 until his death. He was known for his forceful sermons, which were very influential among the colony's leadership. Cotton himself be- came intolerant of religious dissenters. In 1635, he attacked **Roger Williams** (*see*) on the issue of religious freedom and later took part in the banishment of **Anne Hutchinson** (*see*) in 1638. Cotton also sought to make Massachusetts a theocracy (church state). He maintained that the authority of the colony's civil magistrates ought to be extended over the consciences of its citizens. Cotton died on December 23, 1652.

Oliver Cromwell

CROMWELL, Oliver (1599–1658). Cromwell was the leader of a coalition of Parliament supporters and Puritans that defeated **Charles I** (*see*) in the Puritan Revolution during the 1640s. He ruled England as lord protector from 1653 to 1658. During this interregnum, the English colonies in America were allowed to rule themselves with almost no interference. In England, however, Cromwell governed as a dictator, supported by an army. Religious toleration was extended to Jews and all Protestants except Anglicans and **Quakers** (*see*), who were persecuted along with Catholics. In 1657, Parliament offered to make Cromwell king, but he refused. Two years after his death, England installed a constitutional monarchy under **Charles II** (*see*).

D

DAVENPORT, John (1597–1670). One of the founders of the New Haven Colony, Davenport was an Anglican minister who was forced to flee from England to Holland in 1633 because of his nonconformist views. In Holland, Davenport ran into religious differences with the Dutch church. He left after three years and returned briefly to England. There he joined **Theophilus Eaton** (*see*) on an expedition to establish a Puritan settlement in New England. The New Haven Colony was founded in March, 1638. Davenport became pastor of the colony's church and one of its leading figures. In 1655, he helped Governor Eaton to draw up a new code of moralistic laws that became known as the Connecticut Blue Laws. Six years later he unsuccessfully opposed the **Half-Way Covenant** (*see*), which eased church membership requirements. In 1665, he was also unsuccessful in preventing the take-over of the New Haven Colony by the Connecticut Colony under the **Connecticut Charter of 1662** (*see*). As a result, he subsequently decided to accept the pulpit of the First Church of Boston. His departure, without the approval of the New Haven congregation, caused a scandal and divided the Boston congregation. He died in March, 1670, a few months after his arrival in Boston.

DAY, Stephen (1594?–1668). An English locksmith, Day became the first printer in the British colonies. In the summer of 1638, he sailed for New England with the Reverend Jose Glover (?–1638), whose printing press he had contracted to operate for two years. Glover died during the voyage, and Day supervised the setting up of the press in Cambridge, Massachusetts, for Glover's widow. The printing plant, called the Cambridge Press, began operation in 1639. In 1640, the first book printed in the colonies, the *Bay Psalm Book,* was published. Because Day was almost illiterate, some historians maintain that the first printer was really Day's son, Matthew (1620?–1649), who was trained as a printer and whose name appears on an almanac in 1647. However, six years earlier, the father had been granted land because he was "the first that sett upon printing." Day had then left the press to his son to operate and busied himself with acquiring land, prospecting for minerals, and promoting an ironworks. He was briefly imprisoned in 1643 for fraud. Afterward, he returned to his original trade, locksmithing, until his death in December, 1668. His last name is sometimes spelled Daye.

DEERFIELD MASSACRE. *See* **Queen Anne's War.**

DINWIDDIE, Robert (1693–1770). A native of Scotland, Dinwiddie was collector of customs in Bermuda before being appointed in 1738 as surveyor general of customs for the southern ports of North America. As lieutenant governor of Virginia (1751–1758), Dinwiddie insisted that the colonists pay a fee for securing patents to lands they already held. The **House of Burgesses** (*see*) successfully appealed the case. The dispute, however, divided the colony at a time when the French were threatening British power in North America (*see p. 132*). As a result, Dinwiddie was forced to send for British troops to defend the western frontier area (*see* **Edward Braddock**). Dinwiddie met such opposition in his attempts to raise money locally for military operations that he urged Parliament to tax the colonies for their own defense expenses. He retired to England in 1758 and died there on July 27, 1770.

DUDLEY, Joseph (1647–1720). After graduation from Harvard College, which his father, **Thomas Dudley** (*see*), had helped to establish, Joseph Dudley became active in the political life of the Massachusetts Bay Colony. In 1682, he was sent to London to argue against the threatened revocation of the colony's charter. Instead, he secretly advised **Charles II** (*see*) to annul it. The king did, and then chose Dudley as the temporary head of the new colonial government. Dudley later served prominently under his replacement, **Sir Edmund Andros** (*see*). When the Andros government was overthrown by the colonists in 1689, Dudley was recalled to England. For many years afterward he held political posts in England and New York. In 1702, he was appointed governor of Massachu-

Joseph Dudley

setts. Highly unpopular, Dudley encountered constant colonial opposition throughout his term in office. He was finally replaced as governor in 1715 and died in Roxbury on April 2, 1720.

DUDLEY, Thomas (1576–1653). The English-born son of a country gentleman, Dudley immigrated to New England in 1630 with **John Winthrop** (*see*). He served as the first deputy governor of the Massachusetts Bay Colony, a post to which he was elected 13 times. He served four terms as governor of the colony and was its most influential member next to Winthrop. Dudley helped to plan the establishment of Harvard College and signed its charter during his term as governor in 1650. He was the father of **Anne Bradstreet** and **Joseph Dudley** (*see both*). He died in Roxbury on July 31, 1653.

E

EATON, Theophilus (1590–1658). Eaton, a successful London merchant, sponsored the founding of the New Haven Colony by Puritans. Among those he gathered together to immigrate to New England in 1637 was his friend and pastor **John Davenport** (*see*). Eaton selected the site on which New Haven was founded in March, 1638. At a town meeting in June of the next year, the colonists chose the ancient Hebrew laws of Moses as the basis for governing the colony. They limited voting privileges and the holding of office to church members. Eaton was elected governor and reelected every year until his death. By 1643, the New Haven Colony had expanded to include Stamford and Southold, Long Island. This provoked disputes with neighboring

Dutch settlements. Eaton's subsequent effort to establish a fur-trading post on the Delaware River failed because of harassment by the Dutch. His business ventures suffered a second setback in 1646, when a 150-ton cargo vessel built by the colony was lost at sea. Following this, some of the leading settlers left the colony to return to England. Eaton remained, however, and devoted himself to farming. In 1655, after the remaining colonists decided that the Mosaic law was inadequate as a guide to self-government, Eaton and Davenport drew up a new code of laws. These became known as the Connecticut Blue Laws because of the blue paper covers in which they were bound. The laws attempted to enforce strict moral standards by taxing showy clothing, prohibiting almost all non-religious activity on Sunday, and forbidding such pastimes as drinking, smoking, and dancing.

EDWARDS, Jonathan (1703–1758). One of the most eloquent orators of his time, Edwards was a Congregational minister who led the **Great Awakening** (*see*), America's first religious revival, in Massachusetts. The son of a preacher in East Windsor, Connecticut, Edwards entered Yale at the age of 12 and graduated in 1720. He spent the next two years studying for the ministry. During this time, Edwards underwent a religious experience in which he said he was visited by God. He subsequently believed that everyone who wanted to join the church should have a similar experience. In 1726, Edwards became copastor with his grandfather, Solomon Stoddard (1643–1729), of the influential church of Northampton, Massachusetts, and took over the parish on Stoddard's death three years

Jonathan Edwards

later. He lived a strict, simple life, waking up each morning at four o'clock and devoting his day to study, contemplation, and writing. In 1735, when the community was caught up in the Great Awakening, he admitted 30 converts a week to his church. Edwards, at this time, delivered sermons emphasizing that each person was a sinner who could escape eternal damnation only by being converted and leading a pious life. His popularity declined as the religious fervor subsided, and in 1750 his congregation voted to dismiss him in a dispute over church membership. Edwards moved to Stockbridge, Massachusetts, where he preached to settlers and Indians. In 1758, he accepted the presidency of the College of New Jersey (now Princeton University). He arrived there during a smallpox epidemic and developed a fever after being inoculated. He died on March 22, 1758.

ELIOT, John (1604–1690). Known as the Apostle to the Indians, Eliot was a minister who spent most of his life trying to convert the New England tribes to Christianity. Puritan friends induced him to emigrate from England to Boston in 1631. He was subsequently appointed teacher of the church at Roxbury, a post he retained for nearly 60 years. Eliot learned the Indian language and translated the Ten Commandments and the Lord's Prayer. He also preached to the Indians in their own language. In the early 1660s, he published, in the Algonquian language, the first Bible printed in North America. Hoping to "civilize" all Indians in the area, Eliot established a system of self-governing Indian communities. The first village was formed at Natick in 1651. By 1674, there were 14 such villages and about 4,000 "praying Indians," as Eliot's converts were called. During **King Philip's War** (*see*) in the mid-1670s, the converted Indians were loyal to the settlers, but the frightened colonists attacked them anyway. Only four communities survived destruction, and these eventually dwindled away. Eliot spent the remaining years before his death in 1690 trying to revive the Christian faith among the Indians.

ENDECOTT, John (1589?–1665). A Puritan of strict religious beliefs, Endecott founded Salem and served several terms as governor of the Massachusetts Bay Colony. He emigrated from England in 1628 after purchasing, with six other persons, a patent to settle the territories around Massachusetts Bay. He sailed aboard the *Abigail* without waiting for royal confirmation of the patent, which came the following year when **Charles I** (*see*) incorporated the **Massachusetts Bay Company** (*see*). Endecott settled at Naumkeag, a small fishing post established by

Righteous John Endecott has the Maypole at Merry Mount chopped down.

Roger Conant (1592?–1679) and other dissatisfied settlers from Plymouth. While waiting for the main body of colonists to arrive with **John Winthrop** (*see*), Endecott was appointed governor of the "Plantation" in Massachusetts. He renamed Naumkeag "Salem" after the Hebrew word *shalom* (peace) and forced Conant and his followers to submit to his authority. Endecott also ordered **Miles Standish** (*see*) to cut down the Maypole erected at Merry Mount and had the supporters of **Thomas Morton** (*see*) chastised for holding parties there. Later, as governor of the Massachusetts Bay Colony, Endecott persecuted **Quakers** (*see*) and compelled them to leave.

F

FORT DUQUESNE. Several key battles of the **French and Indian War** (*see*) were fought for possession of this French stronghold, built on the site of modern Pitts-

burgh. In an attempt to halt French inroads in the upper Ohio River Valley, the Ohio Company of Virginia in 1753 began construction of a new fort at the spot where the Monongahela and Allegheny Rivers meet to become the Ohio. Early the next year, the French dispatched an army of about 1,000 men from Montreal that evicted the English and erected Fort Duquesne on the cleared British site. In July, 1754, the French struck nearby Fort Necessity and forced George Washington's entrenched troops to surrender. **Edward Braddock** (*see*) led a British force against the fort in 1755, but it was ambushed before it could reach its objective. For the next three years, until the tide of war began to turn against them, the French were sole masters of the Ohio Valley. When a British army led by John Forbes (1710–1759) and Henry Bouquet (1719–1765) drew within striking distance of the fort in November, 1758, the French burned and abandoned it.

FREDERICK II (1712–1786). A liberal monarch who tolerated religious dissent and believed in impartial justice, Frederick was called "the Great" by his Prussian subjects. Five months after he ascended the throne in 1740, he began organizing an army to invade nearby Silesia, which was also claimed by Maria Theresa of Austria (1717–1780). The Austrians were defeated and forced to cede Silesia to Frederick. The conflict widened into a general European war, known as the War of the Austrian Succession (1740–1748). The conflict, known in North America as **King George's War** (see), embroiled British and French forces. It was followed by the **French and Indian War** (see), which involved participants of the Seven Years War (1756–1763) in Europe. Frederick, an outstanding military leader, fought off almost the entire Continent and established Prussia as a major European power. He died on August 17, 1786, after catching cold while reviewing troops in a rainstorm.

FRENCH AND INDIAN WAR (1754–1763). The contest for control of North America took more than 70 years to resolve after the first clash between French and British forces in the winter of 1689–1690 (see pp. 109–121). The French and Indian War was preceded by three indecisive struggles known as **King William's War, Queen Anne's War,** and **King George's War** (see all). All four are now called the French and Indian wars. The conflicts pitted English colonists, who were confined to eastern seaboard settlements, against the French, who blocked English expansion to the west and to the north. The final war was rooted in French attempts to expel British fur traders from the Ohio River Valley. On July 3, 1754, Lieutenant Colonel George Washington, who had been sent to stop the French, was forced to surrender his temporary camp, Fort Necessity. The British suffered a number of other defeats in the first years of the war, the worst of which was the ambush of troops led by **Edward Braddock** near **Fort Duquesne** (see both) in 1755. However, English naval, supply, and numerical superiority slowly began to turn the tide. Key victories were won in 1758 and 1759 at Fort Louisbourg, Fort Frontenac, Fort Duquesne, and Quebec. Montreal, the last French stronghold, fell in 1760. Meanwhile, in Europe, a conflict known as the Seven Years War (1756–1763) had broken out two years after fighting started in North America. Both wars were ended by the Peace of Paris, signed in 1763. France gave Britain all her North American holdings east of the Mississippi, except for New Orleans. From that time, France was virtually finished as a colonial power in the New World.

FRONTENAC, Count Louis de (1620–1698). Twice governor of New France (Canada), Frontenac sought to extend French influence south of the Great Lakes. He actively promoted the explorations of **Robert Cavelier de La Salle, Jacques Marquette,** and **Louis Jolliet** (see all). Little is known of Frontenac's early life other than that his father was an army colonel. Frontenac himself fought with distinction on the Continent before being appointed to govern the colony of New France in 1672. He was an able leader, but his administration was a stormy one. He quarreled with church officials, the ruling sovereign council, and the ministers of **Louis XIV** (see). He was recalled to France in 1682 but was again appointed governor seven years later. He subsequently waged war against the Iroquois and neighboring British colonies (see **King William's War**).

G

GASPEE. A British revenue schooner, the H.M.S. *Gaspee* was burned near Providence, Rhode Island, on June 10, 1772, by colonists seeking to avenge harassment by customs officials (see pp. 165–166). England was determined to curb widespread smuggling in the colonies. Customs ships, among them the *Gaspee* under the command of Lieutenant William Dudingston, were sent to patrol the Atlantic coast. The *Gaspee* began aggressively stopping even small merchant vessels and confiscating their goods. She ran aground on June 9, 1772, on Namquit Point near Pawtucket while chasing another vessel. The next evening, a group of about 150 angry Providence merchants, including **Abraham Whipple** (see), boarded the ship. They shot and wounded Dudingston and captured his men. After putting the officer and crew ashore, the raiders set fire to the *Gaspee* and destroyed her. Colonial officials appointed a Commission of Inquiry to discover and punish those responsible. The accused were to be tried in England. However, Rhode Islanders bitterly opposed the investigation and no evidence could be obtained. No one was ever brought to trial. The burning of the *Gaspee* was one of the first openly warlike acts against the British before the start of the American Revolution.

George II

GEORGE II (1683–1760). George II became king of England on the death of his father, George I (1660–1727). He also became elector of Hanover, a position his father had held, and was more interested in protecting his Hanoverian estates in Germany than in ruling England. As a result, England became involved in the War of the Austrian Succession (1740–1748) against France and Spain. In North America, the conflict was known as **King George's War** (*see*). At the battle of Dettingen in 1743, George became the last English king to lead his troops in person. When Prince Charles Edward Stuart (1720–1788), known as Bonny Prince Charlie, invaded England from Scotland in 1745, George sent his son, the Duke of Cumberland (1721–1765), to crush the rebel Scots, which he did ruth-

lessly at Culloden Moor the following year. Meanwhile, continued clashes between French and colonial forces in America led to the **French and Indian War** (*see*). George II died in 1760, before the end of the war, and was succeeded by his grandson, George III (1738–1820).

GREAT AWAKENING. The series of religious revivals known as the Great Awakening swept the American colonies in the 1730s and 1740s and gave rise to several new religious denominations. By the beginning of the 18th century, religious sentiment had declined significantly in America. Beginning in 1719, a German minister, Theodore Frelinghuysen (1691–1748), conducted meetings in New Jersey's Raritan Valley to rekindle religious spirit in the colonists. The movement soon spread to New England, where a Congregational preacher, **Jonathan Edwards** (*see*), became its leader. Edwards warned his congregation either to repent their sins and lead pious lives or face God's eternal wrath —hellfire and damnation. The Great Awakening reached its peak when George Whitefield (1714–1770), a founder of a Methodist sect, set out in 1739 on a two-year journey throughout the colonies and "saved" thousands of souls. Whitefield's dramatic sermons caused worshipers to shriek, moan, and become physically agitated. Although revivals became infrequent after 1750, the Great Awakening had far-reaching effects. Many persons began going to church again, and the Congregational Church alone gained about 25,000 converts. In addition, a number of new sects were formed. Competition among them resulted in the establishment of new educational institu-

tions. Princeton was founded by Presbyterians in 1746, Columbia by Anglicans in 1754, Brown by Baptists in 1764, and Dartmouth by Congregationalists in 1769.

GRENVILLE, George (1712–1770). Grenville was both prime minister and chancellor of the exchequer (1763–1765) when Parliament passed the **Sugar Act** and the **Stamp Act** (*see both*). The two measures increased the hostility of the American colonists toward the king. Although a competent administrator, Grenville was completely tactless and is considered one of England's poorest statesmen. George III, who disliked him intensely, dismissed Grenville from office in 1765, and he never again held a public post.

H

HALF-WAY COVENANT. By admitting to church membership persons who had not undergone religious conversion, this document helped break down the rigid authority of Congregationalism, which is what the American brand of Puritanism became known as in the 17th century. First-generation Puritans had proudly referred to themselves as Visible Saints, because God had supposedly visited them and said that they were "chosen." About the middle of the 17th century, when the number of parishioners had dwindled considerably, the question arose whether their children were also chosen. The Half-Way Covenant, adopted by the Massachusetts Church Synod in 1662, was a temporary answer. It enabled children to join the church but prohibited them from taking the sacrament of the Last Supper or voting in church matters—

hence the title "Half-Way." The covenant bolstered church attendance. It also enabled a few families to control the government of Massachusetts, because only church members had the right to vote. A century later, any person was permitted to join the Congregational Church and to enjoy full rights as a worshiper.

HARVARD, John (1607–1638). John Harvard was a graduate of Cambridge University in England and immigrated to the Massachusetts Bay Colony in 1637. He settled at Charlestown, where he became a wealthy landowner and a leader in the Puritan Church. Before his arrival in America, about 100 colonists who had attended English universities decided to provide the same quality of education for their sons in America. They obtained money from the Massachusetts Bay Colony in 1636 to establish a college at Cambridge. Harvard took an interest in it soon after reaching America. When he died of tuberculosis on September 14, 1638, he left half of his possessions to help build the school. He also willed it his library of about 400 books. Because Harvard's bequest surpassed any other donation, the General Court of Massachusetts decided to name the school Harvard in his honor.

HENRY, Patrick (1736–1799). A farmer, self-trained lawyer, and an accomplished orator, Henry was a leader of the Virginia frontier settlers in the **House of Burgesses** (*see*). In May, 1765, Henry presented the **Virginia Resolves** (*see*), which challenged England's right to tax the colonies. He played an active role in establishing the **Committees of Correspondence** (*see*). He was also instrumental in setting up the First Continental Congress, which met in Philadelphia in 1774. In 1775, Henry urged Virginians to arm themselves, saying, "I know not what course others may take, but as for me, give me liberty, or give me death." He was twice elected governor of Virginia (1776–1779 and 1784–1786). Henry believed that the American colonies should be governed by a representative body that would be as responsive to the will of the people as practically possible. He opposed the ratification of the United States Constitution because he believed that it would compromise the right of Virginia to govern itself as it saw fit. However, after the Bill of Rights was added to the Constitution, he became a supporter of the federal system of

SHELBURNE MUSEUM

Patrick Henry

government. He declined offers to serve in the United States Senate, on the Supreme Court, and as Secretary of State. He was elected to the Virginia legislature in 1799 but died before taking his seat.

HIGGINSON, Francis (1586?–1630). Higginson founded America's first Puritan Congregational Church at Salem, Massachusetts, in 1629. After being ordained in the Church of England in 1614, Higginson became attracted to the views expounded by **Thomas Hooker** (*see*) and other Puritans. At first, Higginson hoped to reform the Anglican Church without leaving it. The Massachusetts Bay Company persuaded him to sail to New England on the *Talbot* in 1629. He settled at Salem and there came under the influence of the Plymouth Separatists (*see pp. 54–61*). Together with the Reverend Samuel Skelton, Higginson established the Salem church on August 6, 1629. The congregation, in the first written ballot taken in America, elected Skelton pastor and Higginson teacher of the church. Higginson died during the winter of 1630, apparently succumbing to tuberculosis.

HOOKER, Thomas (1586?–1647). Hooker was a Congregationalist clergyman who, with a group of his parishioners, founded a colony in 1636 at what is now Hartford, Connecticut. He had been forced to flee England in 1630 because of his Puritan beliefs. After living in Holland, he migrated to Boston in 1633. Hooker and his friend **Samuel Stone** (*see*) became pastor and teacher, respectively, of a church at New Towne (Cambridge), Massachusetts. Although the church prospered, Hooker resented the autocratic rule of the Puritan magistrates. He sought permission to move elsewhere in the colony, but **John Cotton** (*see*) persuaded the General Court of the Massachusetts Bay Colony to deny the request. Despite this, Hooker, Stone, and about 100 followers left and settled in Connecticut. An early exponent of democracy, Hooker wrote in a sermon in 1638 that "The privi-

The House of Burgesses met in the Virginia Capitol at Williamsburg.

over most of Canada, and an extremely profitable business was conducted with the Indians. A bitter rivalry gradually developed between the company's traders and the French, who sent several expeditions against the British forts. Individual French fur traders also began to encroach upon the company's territories, and in 1787 they combined to form the North-West Fur Company of Montreal. The two rival companies then engaged in such vicious competition that Parliament compelled them to combine in 1821. The company still operates, but without the monopolies it once enjoyed.

lege of election . . . belongs to the people," and that the power of officeholders should have limits. In 1639, these ideas were embodied in the first written colonial constitution, Fundamental Orders of Connecticut, which declared Connecticut an independent commonwealth. Hooker realized a long-time ambition in 1643 when he helped organize the United Colonies of New England, a defensive confederation. About this time, he also wrote a complete exposition of the principles of Congregationalism, entitled *Survey of the Summe of Church Discipline.* Years after Hooker's death in 1647, **Cotton Mather** (*see*) said that his stature was so great he could keep a king in his pocket.

HOUSE OF BURGESSES. The first representative assembly in North America was established in Jamestown, Virginia, in the summer of 1619 and called the House of Burgesses. Its initial members were plantation owners, who were asked to help the governor of the colony and his council to revise the laws of the growing settle-

ment. Under a new constitution in 1621, the burgesses were elected annually from counties, towns, and plantations. They could grant supplies and make new laws, but the governor and council retained veto rights. After the Restoration in England in 1660 (*see* **Charles II**), a bitter struggle developed between the colonists and the English government over the rights of the House of Burgesses. It was settled in 1689, with the colonists keeping the important power to levy taxes. The House of Burgesses was moved to Williamsburg in 1669, when that city was made the capital of Virginia.

HUDSON'S BAY COMPANY. The oldest trading corporation in existence, the Hudson's Bay Company was formed when **Charles II** (*see*) of England granted a charter in 1670 to 18 Englishmen to purchase skins and furs from the Indians of North America. The company held a monopoly over a vast tract of Canada that was drained by the rivers that flow into Hudson Bay. Forts and trading posts were gradually established

HUTCHINSON, Anne (1591–1643). Anne was banished from the Massachusetts Bay Colony in 1638 for her religious beliefs. She was the daughter of a nonconformist minister in England, and after her marriage in 1612 became an admirer of the Puritan preacher **John Cotton** (*see*). She followed him to Boston in 1634 with her husband and children. A deeply pious person, Anne began to express her own religious opinion that salvation came from God's freely given grace and love. She

Anne Hutchinson denied Puritan charges that she held heretical views.

E55

criticized ministers who advocated the Covenant of Works, which held that salvation was only awarded to people who obeyed specific church and civil laws. As a result, Anne was called a traitor and blasphemer. Cotton defended Anne until a Synod of Churches in 1637 denounced her views as heretical. She was tried and found guilty of "traducing the ministers and their ministry." Sentenced to banishment, Anne was allowed to remain in Boston for the winter. She was placed in Cotton's custody and forced to recant her sins. Anne later retracted this confession and was formally excommunicated. She moved with her family and a few of her adherents to Rhode Island in 1638. When her husband died four years later, Anne settled on Long Island Sound. She was killed by Indians near Pelham Bay.

HUTCHINSON, Thomas (1711–1780). Hutchinson, a wealthy merchant born in Boston, was lieutenant governor (1758–1771) and royal governor (1771–1774) of Massachusetts at a time of increasing colonial resentment against England. In 1760, he also became chief justice of Massachusetts for one year. Hutchinson believed that the colonies should be subordinate to Parliament. His efforts to enforce the **Stamp Act** and the **Sugar Act** (*see both*) in 1765 prompted angry Boston citizens to sack and burn his home. Embittered, Hutchinson favored strict measures against colonial disobedience. However, following the **Boston Massacre** (*see*) in 1770, Hutchinson, then the acting governor, withdrew English troops from Boston at the demand of **Samuel Adams** (*see*) in order to avoid further bloodshed. But in 1773, Hutchinson's attempt to un-

This wampum belt symbolized the unity of the five Iroquois nations.

load several cargoes of inexpensive British tea aggravated colonial tempers and led to the **Boston Tea Party** (*see*). Hutchinson went to England in 1774 and died there six years later.

I

IROQUOIS LEAGUE. The largest Indian Empire in the New World is believed to have been established in 1570 by a shaman (mystic) named Deganawidah and his follower, Hiawatha. The league was composed of five "nations"— Cayugas, Mohawks, Oneidas, Onondagas, and Senecas—who spoke a similar language. They called their government the Great Peace because it was designed to end warfare among themselves and to establish an alliance against their enemies. The Iroquois domain extended from present-day Ontario to Virginia and as far west as Michigan and Illinois. By 1675, the Five Nations had conquered most of the smaller Indian tribes in northeastern North America. Another tribe, the Tuscaroras, joined the league in 1722. From then on, the league was known as the Six Nations. The league's members called themselves the People of the Long House after the large wooden structures in which many families lived. The Iroquois fought on England's side

in the colonial wars of the 17th and 18th centuries—first against the French, then against **Pontiac** (*see*). Many of them also fought with the British against the American revolutionaries. In 1779, General John Sullivan (1740–1795) led a force of 5,000 American militiamen against the Iroquois and defeated them. The league, some believe, may have influenced the framers of the United States Constitution. It was based on a federation of tribes that gave up some of their authority to a central governing body. The league, however, was in many ways more progressive than the early American Republic. It banned child labor and capital punishment and permitted women to vote.

J

JAMES II (1633–1701). Before he became king, James II, then the Duke of York, was awarded the colony of New Netherland in 1664 by his brother, **Charles II** (*see*). He renamed the former Dutch possession New York and ruled it tyrannically. As king (1685–1688), James governed England in similar fashion. He ignored the wishes of Parliament, meddled in the affairs of local governments, and aroused fear and resentment by appointing fellow Roman Catholics to powerful state and military positions. His arbitrary and incompetent rule provoked the bitter opposition of both English political parties. Two years after James became king, the leaders of these parties offered the crown to William of Orange (1650–1702), his son-in-law. William sailed from Holland in 1688 and easily routed the king's army. James was captured but was allowed to escape to France. William was crowned as William III. After several unsuccessful attempts to regain his throne, James retired to a life of penance and religious works. He died in France in 1701. The overthrow of James II and the accession of William III and his wife, Mary II (1662–1694), is known as the Glorious Revolution. It marked the victory of Parliament over absolute rule by the king.

JENKINS' EAR, War of (1739–1741). Commercial rivalry between England and Spain was the fundamental cause of the War of Jenkins' Ear. The name came from an incident in 1731, when an English sea captain, Robert Jenkins (dates unknown), tried to encroach on a Spanish trading monopoly in the Caribbean. Jenkins' ship was boarded by the Spanish, who ransacked his cargo and cut off his ear. He took the ear back to England and exhibited it. The incident was largely ignored until 1738, when Jenkins appeared with the severed ear before a committee of the House of Commons. Members of Parliament, eager for war with Spain, used the propaganda effect of Jenkins' ear to declare war on Spain. No major battles took place, and the conflict was merged into the War of the Austrian Succession (*see* **King George's War**).

JOLLIET, Louis (1645–1700). Jolliet, together with **Jacques Marquette** (*see*), led an expedition that discovered the headwaters of the Mississippi River in 1673. Jolliet had been born in the Province of Quebec and at one point considered becoming a Jesuit priest. In 1667, he visited Europe and studied map making for a year. With **Robert Cavelier de La Salle** (*see*), Jolliet was an important force in extending French influence into the Mississippi Valley. He had a talent for dealing with Indians and learned their languages easily. He explored widely in the Great Lakes area beginning in 1669 and later reached as far north as Hudson Bay in 1694. In 1672, officials in New France (Canada) chose Jolliet to find "the great Western river" that so much had been heard about. Marquette was selected as chaplain of the expedition. The two explored the Mississippi to the mouth of the Arkansas, and by returning north along the Illinois and Des Plaines Rivers, became the first white men to visit the site of present-day Chicago. Jolliet's journals and maps were lost in 1674, when his canoe overturned in rapids near Montreal. Hence, Jolliet has not received full credit for his discoveries, because historians have relied on the written records of Marquette. His skill in mapping rivers and waterways resulted in his appointment as royal hydrographer of New France in 1697. His last name is sometimes spelled Joliet.

K

KING GEORGE'S WAR (1744–1748). The third clash between the French and the English for control of North America was an outgrowth of a wider European conflict known as the War of the Austrian Succession (1740–1748). It was one of four colonial wars known as the French and Indian wars (*see pp. 109–121*) and was named for **George II** (*see*) of England. The European conflict began in 1740 when **Frederick II** (*see*) of Prussia invaded Silesia. In North America, the major battle centered on the French fort of Louisbourg (*see pp. 130–131*). Situated at the mouth of Lawrence Bay, the fort was the key to the French defense network in North America and was known as the Gibraltar of the West. Its walls were 40 feet thick and 30 feet high. In 1745, about 4,000 English colonists led by a prosperous merchant named William Pepperell (1696–1759) attacked the fort. A French blunder permitted them to capture a battery of heavy cannon in the harbor. The colonists turned the guns on the fort, finally forcing the French to surrender after nearly two months of siege. When peace was restored in Europe by the Treaty of Aix-la-Chapelle in 1748, Fort Louisbourg was returned to the French in exchange for the city of Madras in India, which the French had captured from the British. The English recaptured the fort during the **French and Indian War** (*see*) in 1758, thus ending France as a New World power.

KING PHILIP'S WAR (1675–1676). A son of the Wampanoag chieftain Massasoit (?–1661), King Philip, whose Indian name was Metacomet, led the Indians of New England in the bloodiest war in the history of that area. The Indians resented the colonists' intrusion on lands the Indians claimed. Massasoit had been friendly with the settlers, but after

In this engraving, a Wampanoag falls in battle during King Philip's War.

his death, the colonists captured his eldest son, Alexander (?–1662), who died in captivity. Philip, now the chief, refused to maintain peace. He was able to form an alliance of several tribes. In 1675, when three Wampanoags were executed for the murder of a Christian Indian, open hostilities broke out. Philip's warriors went on a rampage, attacking frontier outposts, including Deerfield (*see pp. 126–127*), Hadley, Northfield, and Lancaster. They murdered colonists, killed cattle, and burned crops and homes. Soldiers, recruited from the colonies in the Confederation of New England (*see pp. 98–99*), were initially disorganized, ill equipped, and ignorant of Indian tactics. The war did not go well until the English routed the Narragansets of Rhode Island at the Great Swamp Fight on December 19, 1675. The tribes of the Connecticut Valley surrendered the following May. Philip was captured in August, 1676, and shot. His death marked the end of the war in southern New England, though sporadic hostilities in the north continued for many years. Thousands of Indians and settlers were killed in the war. Half the towns in New England suffered some damage, and 16 communities in Massachusetts and four in Rhode Island were completely destroyed. As a result, the westward expansion of white settlers did not resume for 40 years.

KING WILLIAM'S WAR (1689–1697). This was the first of four conflicts between England and France known in North America as the French and Indian wars (*see pp. 109–121*). It was named after William III (1650–1702), who was William of Orange, a Dutch prince who had agreed to become the English king in order to involve England in Holland's struggle with France. Friction between French and English settlers in North America had resulted in several serious clashes prior to 1689. Open warfare erupted in May of that year with the outbreak of hostilities in Europe, where the conflict was called the War of the Grand Alliance. During the first winter, **Count Louis de Frontenac** (*see*), the governor of New France (Canada), destroyed the British fort at Schenectady, New York, and captured two settlements in northern New England. The only English victory was the seizure of Port Royal in **Acadia** (*see*) in 1690, but French troops recaptured it a year later. In 1690, Jacob Leisler (1640?–1691), a rebel colonist who had seized New York, organized a joint land assault on Montreal and a naval expedition against Quebec. Both failed. The English colonies were subjected to a succession of Indian raids along their western frontiers in the mid-1690s, before the **Peace of Ryswick** (*see*) was signed in 1697. War was declared again in 1701 (*see* **Queen Anne's War**).

L

LA SALLE, Robert Cavelier de (1643–1687). La Salle's vision of a great western empire for France led him to explore (1679–1682) the Mississippi to the Gulf of Mexico. He claimed the entire river valley for **Louis XIV** (*see*), naming it Louisiana in his honor. Born near Rouen, France, La Salle had abandoned studies for the clergy to join his brother, a priest, in Montreal in 1666. He was a farmer for two years before turning explorer. In the summer of 1669, he sailed the St. Lawrence River to Lake Ontario, where he

Robert Cavelier de La Salle

met **Louis Jolliet** (*see*). He was twice sent by the governor of New France, **Count Louis de Frontenac** (*see*), in the mid-1670s to seek the French court's approval for expanding the territory of New France. Returning with royal favor, he set sail to explore the lands south of Canada in 1679. At Green Bay, Wisconsin, he sent his fur-laden ship, the *Griffon,* back to Niagara and continued his journey by canoe. (The *Griffon* never arrived, and its fate is unknown.) He founded Fort Crevecoeur on Lake Peoria about 1680. Despite hardships and clashes with the Iroquois, La Salle eventually made his way down the Mississippi and reached the Gulf of Mexico on April 9, 1682. The next year, however, La Salle fell into disfavor when Frontenac was replaced as governor. After traveling to France to regain the favor of the king, La Salle returned to the Gulf of Mexico in 1684 for the purpose of founding a colony at the mouth of the Mississippi. But the expedition could not find the entrance to the Mississippi, and mutiny broke out. La Salle was slain by his own men on the Brazos River in Texas on March 19, 1687.

LOCKE, John (1632–1704). An English philosopher, Locke greatly influenced early American political thought. He believed that man's nature was rational. Locke said that no man had a right to harm another in "life, health, liberty, or possessions." He contended that a government represented a contract drawn up by its citizens and should be guided by the laws of nature, which guaranteed liberty and property. Locke declared that it was the duty of citizens to revolt against a government ruled by tyranny. In

John Locke

1669, he drew up a model constitution for the Carolinas (*see p. 100*). His theory of checks and balances in government was subsequently adopted by the framers of the United States Constitution.

LOUIS XIV (1638–1715). Louis XIV was king of France for 72 years, the longest reign in European history. His power was absolute. In 1667, the French king launched the first of a series of attacks on his European neighbors. Fighting continued almost uninterrupted for the next 48 years, pitting France against Austria, the Netherlands, Spain, and England. During that time, French colonists in North America were involved in two major wars with English colonists (*see* **King William's War, Queen Anne's War**). The first conflict was settled by the **Peace of Ryswick** (*see*) in 1697, which restored to France many of its possessions in North America that had been captured by the English. The second conflict was concluded by the **Treaty of Utrecht** (*see*) in 1713 and 1714, under

which France gave up the Hudson Bay region, New Foundland, and most of **Acadia** (*see*) to England.

M

MARQUETTE, Jacques (1637–1675). Pere (Father) Marquette is probably the best known of the Jesuit missionaries who explored the Midwest of North America during the 17th century. In 1673, seven years after he left France to be posted in Quebec, he and a French trader, **Louis Jolliet** (*see*), set out in search of the "great river" of the West. The explorers went by way of Green Bay, Wisconsin, and finally entered the Mississippi River from one of its northern tributaries on June 17, 1673, thus becoming the first Europeans to reach the upper river. Marquette and Jolliet went by canoe down the uncharted river as far as Arkansas. They turned back on learning that the Mississippi emptied into the Gulf of Mexico, which was held by the Spanish. The arduous voyage left Marquette too weak to return to Quebec with the rest of Jolliet's party. He spent a year recuperating at the mission that another Jesuit, **Claude Jean Allouez** (*see*), had established at De Pere, Wisconsin. In the fall of 1674, Marquette set out for northern Illinois, where he hoped to found a mission among the Illinois Indians. He collapsed during the rough voyage and died soon after reaching the Indian encampment.

MASSACHUSETTS BAY COLONY. *See* **Massachusetts Bay Company.**

MASSACHUSETTS BAY COMPANY. Formed originally as a trading venture in 1629, the Massachusetts Bay Company served as a model for the political organization of the New England colonies. Under its charter, which was granted by **Charles I** (*see*) of England, the company was assured that its colony would be self-governing. The company's governor, **John Winthrop** (*see*), and four shiploads of colonists sailed in 1630 for Massachusetts Bay, finally anchoring at Salem. Within the first year, 13 more ships and 1,300 more colonists arrived. The settlers branched out from the coast to found Watertown, Medford, Dorchester, and Roxbury. The company exercised complete control over the Massachusetts Bay Colony through a governing body called the General Court. Stockholders had to belong to the Puritan Church and be property owners in order to vote in annual elections for governor's assistants (legislators). In 1644, the General Court was divided into two parts. A lower chamber was made up of deputies, and an upper chamber was comprised of assistants who represented the various towns. The company remained neutral during the Puritan Revolution in England (*see* **Oliver Cromwell**). However, after the restoration of royal authority in 1660, it found itself in difficulty with **Charles II** (*see*) for having extended its domain over Maine and New Hampshire without royal consent. It had also refused to grant religious freedom, had coined its own money, and would not recognize Parliament's authority. As a result, the company's charter was revoked in 1684, and the king proceeded to establish Massachusetts as a royal colony.

MASSACRE OF 1770. *See* **Boston Massacre.**

MATHER, Cotton (1663–1728). Cotton Mather is usually remembered as the Massachusetts minister who was responsible for the **Salem witchcraft trials** (*see*). However, he was also the most noted scholar of his generation. He wrote more than 450 works on a variety of religious and secular subjects and owned the second-largest library (almost 4,000 volumes) in the colonies. He was born in Boston, the eldest son of the preacher **Increase Mather** and a grandson of **Richard Mather** (*see both*). He entered Harvard College at the age of 12—the youngest person ever admitted to the school. Because of a bad stammer, Mather studied medicine instead of preparing for the ministry. By 1680, two years after his graduation, his speech had improved, and he joined his father at the Second Church of Boston, where he served until his death. Mather quickly became one of the leading preachers in New England. At the height of his popularity in 1692, he became involved in the Salem witch-hunt. Like others, Mather believed that witches existed. He had studied a number of case his-

Cotton Mather

METROPOLITAN MUSEUM OF ART: BEQUEST OF CHARLES ALLEN MUNN, 1924

torics of persons possessed by the Devil. The publication of his findings and his sermons on the subject helped create the panic that resulted in the executions at Salem. Mather had warned the judges against executing convicted witches. But he made no public protest, and it was not until 1702 that he denounced the injustices of the trials. In their aftermath, Mather's influence declined. He maintained that the church should rule the colony at a time when the settlers' religious fervor had cooled. In addition, his arrogant behavior annoyed many people. Among other things, he would fast and pray for days and also apparently had hallucinations. In the area of social reform, however, Mather was progressive. He helped establish a school for slaves and also tried to rehabilitate the poor. Like his father, Mather attempted to convince colonists during a smallpox epidemic in 1721 that inoculation was safe. It was largely through his efforts that inoculation was practiced in Massachusetts long before it was accepted in Europe.

MATHER, Increase (1639–1723). A Puritan minister and president of Harvard College, Increase Mather was the most influential man of his time in the Massachusetts Bay Colony. Born in Dorchester, Massachusetts, he was the youngest son of **Richard Mather** (*see*). He graduated from Harvard in 1656 and went to Ireland to acquire a master's degree from Trinity College, Dublin. He subsequently preached in England until the Restoration of **Charles II** (*see*) again led to the persecution of Puritans. Three years after returning to America in 1661, Mather became the minister of the Second Church of Boston, where he was later assisted by his son, **Cotton Mather** (*see*). After first refusing the presidency of Harvard, he finally took the position in 1685, adding his college duties to his ministerial functions. As president, he encouraged scientific study in addition to promoting Harvard's basic purpose—the training of ministers. Mather entered politics after the charter of the Massachusetts Bay Colony was revoked (*see* **Massachusetts Bay Company**). He went to England in 1688 with a list of colonial grievances to appeal to the king. Two years later, Mather received a new charter from William III (1650–1702). It granted the colonists the concessions they sought, including abolishment of the law that restricted the vote to church members. Upon Mather's return home in 1692, his popularity began to wane. He was accused by some people of encouraging the **Salem witchcraft trials** (*see*). Actually, he was an outspoken critic of the trials and helped to end the executions. His opponents continued their attacks and finally forced Mather to choose between the Harvard presidency and his church ministry. He decided to leave Harvard in 1701 and devote his remaining years to his Boston church. Among the 130 works Mather wrote, his *Discourse Concerning Comets* is a classic of early American science.

MATHER, Richard (1596–1669). Mather was a Puritan minister who founded the so-called Mather Dynasty in Massachusetts. He was a coauthor in 1640 with **John Eliot** (*see*) and the Reverend Thomas Weld (1595–1661) of the *Bay Psalm Book*, the earliest surviving work published in the colonies. Forbidden to preach in England after 1633 because of his

Richard Mather

religious beliefs, Mather immigrated to Massachusetts in 1635. The following year he became teacher of the church at Dorchester, a post he retained until his death. Mather devoted a major portion of his life to organizing the Congregational Church in Massachusetts. A pragmatic individual, he realized that the future of Congregationalism depended upon the acceptance of more people into the church. He drafted the **Half-Way Covenant** (*see*), which extended church membership in 1662. Mather died on April 22, 1669. He was the father of **Increase Mather** and the grandfather of **Cotton Mather** (*see both*).

MONTCALM, Marquis Louis Joseph de (1712–1759). Montcalm, a career soldier, was commander of French forces in North America during the **French and Indian War** (*see*). In 1756, he captured the English outpost at Oswego, New York, thereby returning control of the Lake Ontario region to the French. In 1757, he led a successful attack on Fort William Henry, the British stronghold at the southern end of Lake George in upper New York (*see pp. 114–115*). In July of the

following year, Montcalm's 3,800-man army successfully defended Ticonderoga against a British force numbering 15,000. During the subsequent British siege of Quebec (*see pp. 118–119*), Montcalm was wounded on the Plains of Abraham, outside the city. He died on September 14, 1759, shortly before Quebec fell. The British commander, **James Wolfe** (*see*), died in the same battle.

MORTON, Thomas (1590–1646). Morton was a fun-loving, English-born lawyer who drove his Pilgrim neighbors to despair. In 1626, he assumed control of a colony in what is now Quincy, Massachusetts, after most of its settlers had moved to Virginia. Renamed Merry Mount, the colony became a stiff competitor to the Pilgrims' fur trade. Morton also angered the Pilgrims by ignoring their strict rules against drinking and dancing. On May 1, 1627, Morton and his fellow townsmen erected a tall Maypole topped by a pair of antlers. A party followed in which the settlers danced around it. The Pilgrims considered the Maypole an idol to an evil god and accused the settlers of "beastly practices." They sent **Miles Standish** (*see*) to arrest Morton and deport him to England. The Pilgrims then went to Merry Mount, chopped down the Maypole, and changed the settlement's name to Mount Dagon. Morton briefly returned to the colonies in 1629, only to be sent again to England, where he spent a term in jail. In 1637, he wrote *New England Canaan,* a book in which he poked fun at the Pilgrims. In 1643, he again returned to New England, where he was fined and imprisoned for a year in a Boston jail. He died, poverty-stricken, in Maine in 1646.

N

NAVIGATION ACTS. The purpose of these laws, enacted between 1650 and 1773, was to force the colonies to trade exclusively with England and use only British ships. This policy, known as mercantilism (*see pp. 44–45*), was designed to ensure both a source of raw materials for British factories and a market for their products. The acts did in fact help protect America's infant economy by providing an outlet for its goods. However, as the colonies prospered, many of the colonists began to resent the trade restrictions. Some turned to smuggling. The English reacted by trying to enforce the Navigation Acts more strictly. This, in turn, increased the resentment of the colonists (*see Gaspee*). Their hostility to the acts, together with irritation over the **Sugar Act** and the **Stamp Act** (*see both*), eventually led to the series of conflicts that precipitated the American Revolution.

NEW ENGLAND COMPANY. *See* **White, John.**

NEW HAVEN COLONY. *See* **Eaton, Theophilus.**

NOWELL, Increase (1590–1655). One of the founding officers of the **Massachusetts Bay Company** (*see*), Nowell arrived in the New World in 1630 aboard the *Arbella* (*see*). He became ruling elder of the colony later that year but resigned after two years because he disapproved of church control of the local government (*see pp. 174–176*). Nowell subsequently served as commissioner of military affairs and was secretary of the Massachusetts Bay Colony from 1644 to 1649.

O

OGLETHORPE, James Edward (1696–1785). Oglethorpe was an English humanitarian who founded Georgia as a refuge for debtors and religious minorities. After his election to the House of Commons in 1722, he became interested in the plight of debtors and the grim conditions of their imprisonment. His plan to establish a settlement for them and for persecuted Protestants coincided with England's desire to set up a colony between South Carolina and Spanish Florida. In 1732, Oglethorpe and 19 associates were granted a 21-year charter to be trustees of the Georgia Colony, which was named after **George II** (*see*). Upon his arrival the following year with 116 colonists, Oglethorpe established friendly relations with the Creek Indians and obtained from them the land on which Savannah was founded on February 12, 1733. He subsequently trained an army that ended the Spanish threat to England's southern colonies in 1742, at the Battle of Bloody Marsh. However, his rigid control of colonial affairs irritated many settlers. After his unsuccessful attacks on the Spanish at St. Augustine during **King George's War** (*see*), the colonists brought charges of mismanagement against him. He was recalled to England in 1743, where the charges were later dismissed. Oglethorpe never returned to Georgia. He declined an offer to head the British army in America in 1775.

OTIS, James (1725–1783). Otis was a leading defender of colonial rights in the years before the American Revolution. He was born in Massachusetts and studied law after graduating from Harvard in 1743. He settled in Boston and soon distinguished himself as an attorney. He became the king's advocate general in 1760 but quit the same year rather than defend the Writs of Assistance proposed by the British government. These writs empowered customs officers to search colonial homes for smuggled goods without specific court approval. In February, 1761, when the legality of the writs was debated before the Massachusetts superior court, Otis spoke in opposition. He used the occasion to discuss the relationship between the colonists in America and the home government in England. John Adams (1735–1826), the future President, who took notes on Otis' speech, declared, "American independence was then and there born." Although Otis lost the case, he went on to argue it before the higher Massachusetts General Court, to which he was elected in May of 1761. The General Court subsequently reversed the earlier ruling. In 1762, he began writing a series of pamphlets that became increasingly anti-British, although he stopped short of advocating armed rebellion. In

James Otis is hailed for his attack on the British Writs of Assistance.

1765, Massachusetts sent Otis as a representative to the Stamp Act Congress held in New York to protest taxation by the British. In September, 1769, he publicly denounced the Boston customs officers who had accused him of treason in their reports to England. Meeting these officials in a tavern the next night, Otis got into a brawl and received a head wound. This injury may have caused the insanity that plagued him almost continuously the rest of his life. Otis' role in the Revolution was limited to the time he rushed madly into the line of fire during the Battle of Bunker Hill in 1775 and somehow escaped unscathed. He was killed by lightning on an Andover, Massachusetts, farm on May 23, 1783.

P

PEACE OF RYSWICK. The first phase of the struggle between England and France for possession of North America (*see* **King William's War**) ended in 1697 with the Peace of Ryswick. Signed in the autumn of that year by most European powers, the treaty temporarily halted the invading armies of **Louis XIV** (*see*) of France. He was forced to give up the territories in Europe that France had acquired by force since 1670. In exchange, several captured French possessions in North America, including **Acadia** (*see*), were returned to France. The treaty resolved none of the disputes that had sparked the war, and in 1701 war broke out again (*see* **Queen Anne's War**).

PENN, William (1644–1718). A Quaker and political liberal, Penn helped found three American colonies—Pennsylvania, New Jersey, and Delaware. He joined the Society of Friends, or **Quakers** (*see*), while managing his family's estates in Ireland in the late 1660s. He soon became a leader of the sect and was jailed for a time because of his beliefs. After inheriting most of his father's money in 1670, Penn went on the first of three missionary journeys he made to Holland and Germany. Many of his converts later settled in Pennsylvania. In 1677, Penn drafted a charter, Concessions and Agreements, for a group of Quakers who were immigrating to New Jersey. It provided for a democratic form of government and included a bill of rights that guaranteed religious freedom and other personal liberties. In 1681, he received from **Charles II** (*see*) a large tract of land, which he named Pennsylvania after his father. The following year, he obtained proprietary rights to Delaware. He led a group of colonists to Pennsylvania in 1682 and wrote the colony's constitution, which was similar to the New Jersey charter. It also contained a provision for future amendments, which Penn granted over the years. Penn planned the city of Phila-

William Penn

delphia and negotiated a series of treaties with the Indians. He dealt fairly with the Indians, paying them for their lands and protecting them from exploiters. Penn returned to England in 1684 to settle a border dispute with Maryland and remained there for 15 years. Because of his friendship with **James II** (*see*), he was suspected of treason by James' successor, William III (1650–1702). His charter privileges were revoked in 1692. After he agreed to fortify Pennsylvania against the French —an act that dismayed the peace-loving Quakers—Penn's charter was reissued in 1694. He returned to Pennsylvania in 1699, but by 1701 he was back in England to argue against Parliament's efforts to take over control of all the colonies. In 1712, Penn suffered a stroke and was no longer able to manage his affairs. He died in England on July 30, 1718.

PEQUOTS. The Pequot Indians were an Algonquian tribe that was wiped out by the Puritans. Under pressure from English settlers, the Indians had been forced to move from northern New England into Connecticut, Rhode Island, and Long Island. In 1636, the Pequot War broke out when the Indians murdered a colonial trader. After several indecisive battles, the Puritans assembled a combined force of settlers and Indians of other tribes in 1638. This group trapped 700 Pequots in a village near the mouth of the Mystic River in Connecticut. After setting fire to the village, the Puritans shot into the screaming men, women, and children. Few of the Pequots survived the massacre. Males who were captured were sent to the West Indies and sold as slaves. The chief of the Pequots, Saccacus, managed to escape and

This woodcut of 1638 shows the Pequots besieged in their circular fort.

sought refuge with the Mohawks. But the Mohawks, as a gesture of friendship to the colonists, killed Saccacus and sent his scalp to them. Herman Melville, in his famous novel *Moby-Dick* (1851), named the whaling ship *Pequod* after the extinct tribe.

PITT, William (1708–1778). One of England's ablest statesmen, Pitt won for Britain the dominions of Canada and India and extended the western boundaries of the American colonies to the Mississippi River. He later became an outspoken critic of British policies in the colonies. Pitt was known as "the Elder" to distinguish him from his brilliant son William "the Younger" (1759–1806). The father was named secretary of state in 1757, a year after the Seven Years War began. The British had not been winning, but Pitt,

by emphasizing the use of sea power, changed the course of the war. Ultimately, France was forced to turn over all her North American possessions to England (*see* **French and Indian War**). Shortly before the war ended, George III (1738–1820) became king and forced Pitt to resign. Pitt was convinced that the American colonists would live peacefully under English rule if they were treated fairly. He was instrumental in bringing about the repeal of the **Stamp Act** (*see*) in 1766. He remained an opponent of the king's colonial policies until his death on May 11, 1778. Five years later, Pitt the Younger became the British prime minister at the age of 22.

PONTIAC (1720?–1769). Pontiac, an Ottawa chieftain, led a large alliance of Indians in attacks on

English outposts in the 1760s. He planned to drive out the British settlers who were moving into the Ohio Valley and the Great Lakes region. This area was secured by England in 1763 in the treaty ending the **French and Indian War** (*see*). The Indians were angry because the British took over Indian land and refused to give them free ammunition, as the French had done. When an initial attack on Detroit failed on May 10, 1763, Pontiac laid siege to both Detroit and Fort Pitt, but the garrisons held firm and eventually repelled the Indians. The Indians then launched simultaneous assaults on 12 British strongholds west of the Allegheny Mountains. Eight of the forts fell. A British force sent against Pontiac was defeated in the Battle of Bloody Run near Detroit on July 31, 1763. Peace attempts in 1764 by the British failed, and Pontiac's braves resumed raiding the frontier settlements. Finally, Sir William Johnson (1715–1774), the superintendent of Indian affairs who had promoted an alliance between the **Iroquois League** (*see*) and the British colonists, was able to arrange a peace settlement. Pontiac signed the new treaty on July 25, 1766. Three years later, he was murdered by an Indian who, some believe, was in the employ of an English trader.

PYNCHON, William (1590?–1662). Pynchon was one of the founders of both Roxbury and Agawam (Springfield), Massachusetts. An original officer of the **Massachusetts Bay Company** (*see*), he emigrated from England to Massachusetts in 1630. For many years, Pynchon was a member of the colony's board of assistants, and he served as its treasurer from 1632 to 1634. In 1639, he was appointed magistrate at Springfield, which was renamed for his home in England. Pynchon resettled in England in 1652 after he was denounced as a heretic for the anti-Puritan religious views expressed in his 1650 book, *The Meritorious Price of Our Redemption* (*see pp. 174–176*). He left his property and business interests in Springfield to his son John (1626?–1703) and other members of his family.

Q

QUAKERS. Settlers belonging to the Quakers (the Society of Friends) came to America to escape religious persecution. The sect was founded in England about 1650 by George Fox (1624–1691), who taught that the spirit of God resided in the heart of every man. Fox's followers were resented because, among other things, they refused to worship in the Church of England, bear arms, or take oaths. They also refused to address officials or noblemen by their titles. Two of Fox's women disciples migrated to Massachusetts in 1656, but the Puritans banned them from Boston and also passed laws prohibiting other Quakers from settling in the colony. Undaunted, Quaker missionaries continued to arrive. Many were whipped or fined. Between 1659 and 1661, four Quakers were hanged in Boston. Friends, as they called themselves, settled without opposition on Cape Cod and Long Island in 1657. In 1661, the liberal colony of Rhode Island (*see* **Roger Williams**) permitted them to hold their yearly meeting at Newport. By the time Fox visited America in the early 1670s, Quakers were living throughout the English colonies. Meanwhile, in England, where Quakers were still persecuted, plans were made for a large-scale migration to America. **William Penn** (*see*), a wealthy convert, received a grant of land on the Delaware River from **Charles II** (*see*), which was named Pennsylvania in honor of Penn's father. Penn led a group of Quakers to the province in 1682. The Quakers worshiped without formal rituals, sacraments, music, or art in their churches. They met silently, unless someone wanted to speak or pray. They established schools and insane asylums, worked for prison reforms, and were one of the first groups to denounce slavery. During the 18th century, the Quakers took less and less part in public life and became known as the peculiar people. The simple way they dressed and spoke helped to set them apart from their neighbors. They refused to become involved in the **French and Indian War** (*see*) and instead tried to negotiate a peace treaty with the Indians. Few Quakers participated in the Revolution, but most supported independence. After the war, many Quakers moved west to the slave-free lands of the Northwest Territory, north of the Ohio River.

QUEEN ANNE'S WAR (1701–1713). Queen Anne's War was the English title given to the War of the Spanish Succession. It was named after Queen Anne (1665–1714) and was the second of four colonial wars that became known as the French and Indian wars (*see pp. 109–121*). France and England, rivals for power in North America, had been unable to resolve basic differences following the first of the conflicts, **King William's War** (*see*). Four

Unless one of them wanted to speak, the Quakers worshiped in silence.

years after the **Peace of Ryswick** (*see*) was signed in 1697, war broke out again when the grandson of **Louis XIV** (*see*) of France accepted the Spanish throne. The conflict pitted France against England, the Netherlands, and the Holy Roman Empire. In North America, the colony of New York was reluctant at first to join the war against French Canada because many colonists were engaged in a profitable fur trade with French trappers. Meanwhile, the French and their Indian allies made many attacks along the New England frontier. The most noted raid, the Deerfield Massacre (*see pp. 126–127*), took place on February 29, 1704. During a surprise attack at dawn on the Massachusetts settlement, 53 colonists were killed, and more than 100 were captured. The English settlers retaliated with several attacks on Port Royal, in **Acadia** (*see*), finally capturing it in 1710 with the aid of British troops. In 1711, England sent a naval expedition to seize Quebec. However, 10 of the ships were wrecked, and more than 900 seamen were lost in the attempt. In the same year, negotiations to end the war began in Europe. It officially ended with the signing of the **Treaty of Utrecht** (*see*) in 1713–1714.

R

ROWLANDSON, Mary (1635?–1678?). The wife of a Massachusetts minister-farmer, Mary Rowlandson published her experiences as an Indian captive, and her story became one of the most widely read books of 17th-century America. Like other accounts written by former Indian captives, the book did much to increase the colonists' hatred of the Indians.

When the moon was full, witches—it was suspected—danced in a circle.

Mary was the daughter of one of the founders of Lancaster, a frontier settlement in central Massachusetts. She married Joseph Rowlandson about 1656. During **King Philip's War** (*see*) in the mid-1670s, Narraganset Indians attacked and burned Lancaster, kidnapping Mary and her three surviving children. The Indians took Mary with them as they fled from colonial forces into southern New Hampshire. Her youngest child soon died from exposure. Mary did not undergo the usual torture, apparently because of her ability to make shirts and knit stockings, which she did for the Indians. Her husband was able to ransom her after 82 days of captivity and also secured the release of their two remaining children. Mary's account of her terrible ordeals was first published in 1682 and was reprinted in more than 30 editions.

S

SALEM WITCHCRAFT TRIALS. The Salem witchcraft trials, held from May to September, 1692, were an outgrowth of a general belief in the 17th century in the existence of witches—individuals who had sold their souls to the Devil in exchange for wealth or certain evil powers over other persons. In all, 14 women and six men were executed in 1692. Their accusers were mostly children, some of whom were probably epileptics whose convulsions were taken as a sign that they had been bewitched. The fear of witches reached panic proportions in the Massachusetts village of Salem after a teen-age girl had an argument with a washerwoman. The next day, the girl had convulsions and complained of pains all over her body. When her younger brother and sister also complained of pains, the washerwoman was brought to trial on the suspicion of being a witch. She protested her innocence but was convicted and hanged. Within a few days, a similar incident involved a West Indian slave named Tituba. Beaten until she confessed, Tituba identified nine other witches and was later executed. The mass hysteria that resulted was increased by sermons preached by **Cotton Mather** (*see*) and other ministers. Sir William Phips (1651–1695), the governor of Massachusetts, set up a special court and appointed nine judges—among them **Samuel Sewall** (*see*)—to deal with the crisis. Pressured by public demands for harsh measures, the judges based their convictions almost entirely on "spectral evidence"—the unconfirmed testimony (based on dreams or hallucinations) of allegedly bewitched witnesses. The hysteria reached such extremes that two dogs were actually convicted and executed. Only after Salem's most prominent citizens, including Mather's relatives and Phips' wife, were accused did the court begin to question seriously the use of spectral evidence. When the special court was dissolved in the fall of 1692, 150 prisoners awaiting trial were released, and charges against 200 suspected witches were dropped. In 1771, the General Court of Massachusetts granted payments to the families of the executed victims. The Salem episode has remained a popular theme in American literature. Arthur Miller's play *The Crucible,* which was first produced on Broadway in 1953, is based on the trials.

SALTONSTALL, Richard (1610?–1694). Born in Yorkshire, Saltonstall accompanied his father, Sir Richard Saltonstall (1586–1658?), to Massachusetts in 1630. They were among the founders of both Boston and Watertown. The family returned to England in 1631, and Saltonstall studied law there. His father never went back to Massachusetts, but in 1635 Saltonstall settled at Ipswich, where he played an important role in local affairs. In between three more trips to England, he held several important positions in the colonial government. Like his father (*see pp. 174–176*), Saltonstall opposed the rigidity of the Puritan control of the colony, with its church-dominated government. In 1645, he made a formal protest against the slave trade. In 1672, Saltonstall returned to England, where he died.

SEWALL, Samuel (1652–1730). Sewall was the only one of nine judges in the **Salem witchcraft trials** (*see*) who later publicly repented his role in the executions. Born in England, he came to Boston with his family in 1661. After his graduation from Harvard College in 1671, he tutored at the college for a number of years before becoming the manager of the Massachusetts Bay Colony's printing press, a deputy to the General Court, and a member of the governor's council. Although he had no legal training, Sewall was appointed one of the special commissioners to conduct the witchcraft trials in 1692. Twenty persons were executed by the court. Five years later, on a day of fasting by the colonists in observance of this tragedy, Sewall publicly confessed his error and guilt. By this time he was a judge of the Massachusetts superior court. In 1718, he was made chief justice, a position he held for 10 years. Sewall was one of the first colonists to denounce slavery. He also advocated humane treatment of the Indians, suggesting that they be placed on reservations and schooled in English customs. His *Diary,* written between 1674 and 1729, is the most complete personal record of life in early colonial America that has survived.

SONS OF LIBERTY. Secret organizations of colonists who called themselves Sons of Liberty were formed in 1765 in opposition to the **Stamp Act** (*see*). They took the name from a speech before the House of Commons by Isaac Barré (1726–1802), a British colonel, in which he opposed the taxation of American colonies. The Sons of Liberty viewed themselves as the enforcers of unofficial colonial governments set up

without the crown's approval. They threatened British officials, organized street brawls (*see* **Boston Massacre**), issued decrees, and sponsored revolutionary rallies. They were often supported by wealthy merchants who did not like paying taxes to England. One of their major achievements was to force all tax agents in the colonies to resign before the Stamp Act went into effect. They also burned the home of the lieutenant governor, **Thomas Hutchinson** (*see*). On December 16, 1773, the Sons of Liberty in Massachusetts, led by **Samuel Adams** (*see*), staged the **Boston Tea Party** (*see*). On April 22, 1774, the Sons of Liberty in New York also dressed as Indians and raided a vessel, dumping its cargo of tea into the harbor. That same year, the Sons of

A Stamp Act riot

Liberty carried the news of the formation of the First Continental Congress in Philadelphia to all the colonies.

SPANISH SUCCESSION, War of the. *See* **Queen Anne's War.**

STAMP ACT. The Stamp Act, passed by Parliament in 1765, placed a tax on such items as co-

The Stamp Act inspired this dire warning in a Pennsylvania journal.

lonial newspapers, licenses, almanacs, dice, and playing cards. The revenues from the tax were to help pay for the cost of keeping British soldiers in the American colonies. The act immediately caused an unprecedented amount of protest. In Virginia, **Patrick Henry** (*see*) denounced it in the **House of Burgesses** (*see*). He introduced the **Virginia Resolves** (*see*), in which he challenged England's right to tax the colonies. The **Sons of Liberty** (*see*) forced all colonial stamp agents to resign before the effective date of the tax. Angered by both the Stamp Act and the restrictive **Sugar Act** (*see*) of a year earlier, the colonists united and refused to buy British goods. As a result of the boycott, British exports to America decreased drastically. Parliament, concerned about the loss of trade and the possibility of an open rebellion, repealed the Stamp Act in 1776.

STANDISH, Miles (1584?–1656). Standish was a professional English soldier who was hired by the Pilgrims to accompany them to America. He sailed on the *May-*

flower and was with the small advance party that landed on Plymouth Rock in 1620. A short, stocky man of violent temper, Standish was nicknamed Captaine Shrimpe by **Thomas Morton** (*see*), whose nearby settlement at Merry Mount he broke up. Standish was the only man among the Pilgrims with extensive experience in camping, fieldcraft, and military matters. He and **William Brewster** (*see*) nursed the colonists through their terrible first winter, when all the others fell seriously ill. Standish's own wife, Rose, died. He also handled the colonists' relations with the Indians, whose languages he learned, and he designed and built the Pilgrims' fort. Standish married Rose's sister Barbara in 1624. There is no historical evidence that his friend **John Alden** (*see*) courted Priscilla Mullens on Standish's behalf as related in *The Courtship of Miles Standish* (1858), by Henry Wadsworth Longfellow. The poem's most famous passage reads, *"Archly the maiden smiled, and, with eyes overrunning with laughter, / Said, in a tremulous voice, 'Why don't you speak for yourself, John?' "* Standish returned to England in 1625 to plead for the Pilgrims' right to land and prop-

Miles Standish's sword

erty in the New World. He was one of the eight so-called Undertakers who assumed responsibility for the colonial debt in 1627. He and Alden later founded the town of Duxbury in 1631. Standish died there on October 3, 1656. His first name is sometimes spelled Myles.

STONE, Samuel (1602–1663). A Puritan preacher, Stone negotiated the purchase of the site of Hartford, Connecticut, from the Indians. He had immigrated to Massachusetts in 1633 with **Thomas Hooker** (*see*). The two men shared pastoral functions at the church of New Towne (Cambridge). After moving their congregation to Connecticut in 1636, the ministers took charge of the church at Hartford (named after Stone's birthplace, Hertford, England). In 1637, Stone served as chaplain in the war against the **Pequots** (*see*). On several occasions, he determined the guilt or innocence of witchcraft suspects and advised in civil matters. In the latter part of his life, Stone, a conservative on matters of church membership and the rights of parishioners, became embroiled in a religious controversy. Stone wrote that the heart of Congregationalism was "*a speaking* Aristocracy *in the Face of a silent* Democracy." Connecticut citizens supported him. But in other parts of New England the tide had already turned against him with the adoption in 1662 of the **Half-Way Covenant** (*see*), a document that eased the church's membership restrictions. Stone died on July 20, 1663.

SUGAR ACT. The Sugar Act of 1764 was the first law passed by Parliament to raise money in the colonies for the direct benefit of the crown. The Sugar Act was also aimed at curtailing colonial smuggling activities. Merchants in New England illegally imported foreign molasses from French plantations in the West Indies and turned it into rum for sale abroad (*see* **triangular trade**). This angered British planters in the West Indies, who wanted a monopoly on the American sugar market. Under the Sugar Act, customs duties on British sugar imports were set lower than the duties on non-British imports. Under the new law, ships that did not pay the tax were seized and their cargoes confiscated. The Sugar Act of 1764 and the **Stamp Act** (*see*) of 1765 produced violent protests in the colonies. In 1766, Parliament repealed the Stamp Act and amended the Sugar Act to reduce the tax on foreign imports to the lower level set for British imports.

T

TAYLOR, Edward (1645?–1729). Taylor was an English-born Puritan minister and physician who is often described today as the finest colonial poet of his time. However, his verses, which are religious in theme, were unknown to his contemporaries because Taylor did not publish them. The manuscripts were donated to Yale University by his grandson, Ezra Stiles (1727–1795), a president of the school. The poems remained unknown until 1937, when some of them were discovered with an old manuscript in the Yale library. These were first published in 1939.

TOWNSHEND ACTS. In 1767, Parliament hurriedly passed four acts aimed at reasserting Britain's authority over her American colonies and raising revenues through new taxes. The acts were drawn up by the chancellor of the exchequer and acting head of government, Charles Townshend (1725–1767). They served to increase the anger of colonists who were already incensed over the **Sugar Act** of 1764 and the **Stamp Act** of 1765 (*see both*). The first Townshend Act directed the New York Assembly to enforce the Quartering Act of 1765, which required colonists to provide housing for English soldiers. The second and third acts imposed new import duties on the colonists and created a special board in Boston to regulate and enforce the tax collections. The fourth act abolished the duty on English tea, thus allowing English traders to undersell American merchants (*see pp. 164–165*). Colonial opposition to the acts forced the British to dispatch troops to Boston. One of the regiments that was sent was later involved in the **Boston Massacre** (*see*) in 1770. Later that same year, Parliament repealed all but the tea tax. There were no more incidents until 1773, when the **Sons of Liberty** (*see*) emptied the cargo of a British ship in Boston Harbor (*see* **Boston Tea Party**).

TREATY OF AIX-LA-CHAPELLE. *See* **King George's War.**

TREATY OF UTRECHT. England was given control over **Acadia** (*see*), New Foundland, and the Hudson Bay region under terms of the Treaty of Utrecht, which

The Sugar Act cut off trade with French plantations in the West Indies.

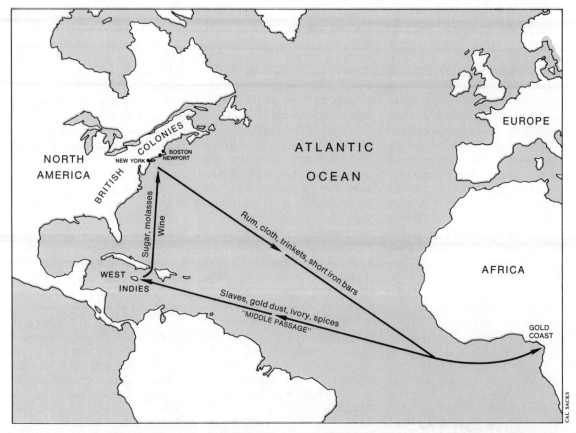

Americans evaded British laws through the triangular trade, bartering rum for slaves and slaves for molasses.

concluded the War of the Spanish Succession, or **Queen Anne's War** (*see*), as it was known in North America. In effect, the treaty was a series of agreements drawn up by representatives of France, Spain, England, Austria, and several other European nations who met in the Dutch city of Utrecht from January, 1712, through September, 1714. Acadia, as French Nova Scotia was then called, had been captured by the English in 1690 during **King William's War** (*see*) but had been returned to France in 1697 under terms of the **Peace of Ryswick** (*see*).

TRIANGULAR TRADE. In order to evade British laws restricting colonial commerce and industry, merchants in the American col-

onies developed a system of smuggling known as the triangular trade (*see p. 156*). Generally, the three points of the triangle were a port on the Atlantic coast, such as Boston, Newport, or New York; a port on the Gold Coast of Africa; and a port in the West Indies, often Kingston or Jamaica. Vessels sailed from America carrying rum, cloth, trinkets, and short iron bars that African natives used for currency. The goods were exchanged for slaves, gold dust, ivory, and spices. The trip from Africa to the West Indies was known as the middle passage, on which many slaves died or fell ill. After selling the slaves, the ship captains purchased molasses, sugar, wines, and other goods, usually from French traders, for

the final leg of the voyage back to the American colonies. The system, which was also known as the three-cornered or roundabout trade, flourished in the 18th century, especially in the northern colonies. It encouraged local industries, trading between the colonies, and the development of a sizable merchant fleet. Parliament tried to stop the smuggling by enacting the Molasses Act of 1733 and the more restrictive **Sugar Act** (*see*) of 1764.

TUSCARORA WAR (1711–1713). This war was fought in eastern North Carolina between several tribes of the Tuscarora Indians, led by Chief Hancock, and neighboring Carolina colonists. Angered by the practices of white traders and intrusions into their hunting grounds, the Tuscaroras opened the war with a brutal attack in September, 1711, that almost wiped out the colonists. Two expeditions were sent from South Carolina to fight the Indians, while colonists in New York and Virginia persuaded potential Indian allies of the Tuscaroras to remain neutral. The first expedition, lasting from January through April of 1712, ended in a truce that was soon broken. The second expedition, consisting of about 30 colonists and 1,000 Indian allies, decisively defeated the Tuscaroras at Fort Nohoroco, near present-day Snow Hill, in March,

Before attacking white settlers in 1711, Tuscaroras hold a war dance.

1713. Following the war, most of the Tuscaroras moved north and eventually became the sixth nation of the **Iroquois League** (*see*). The defeat of the Tuscaroras opened the way for colonial expansion in North Carolina.

V

VANE, Sir Henry (1613–1662). Vane was only 22 years old when he emigrated from England to the Massachusetts Bay Colony in late 1635. Eight months later, he was elected governor of the colony. His term was marked by religious unrest. Vane sided with **Anne Hutchinson** (*see*) in her dispute with **John Winthrop** (*see*) and was defeated by Winthrop in the election of 1637. He returned to England the same year and later served as a member of Parliament under **Oliver Cromwell** (*see*). After the Restoration of **Charles II** (*see*), Vane was convicted of treason. He was executed on June 14, 1662.

VASSALL, William (1592–1655). A founding officer of the **Massachusetts Bay Company** (*see*), Vassall arrived in the New World in 1630 aboard the ***Arbella*** (*see*). He disapproved of the colonial government's dominance in political and religious matters, and he believed that the colony should have been governed according to English law.

VIRGINIA RESOLVES. The Virginia Resolves were seven resolutions introduced in the **House of Burgesses** (*see*) in May, 1765, by **Patrick Henry** (*see*). The resolutions set forth Henry's belief that the colonists had the right to govern themselves. Under the most famous of the resolutions—the fifth resolve—Parliament would have been denied the right to tax the Virginia colonists. However, the House of Burgesses modified this to a policy of no taxation without representation—that is, the colonists believed they should not pay taxes levied by Parliament unless they were represented by a delegate in Parliament. Although the House of Burgesses adopted the modification and only four of Henry's other resolutions, all were printed in newspapers and circulated throughout the other British colonies, sometimes without the revisions that were made. They served as a challenge to other colonial legislatures to adopt similar statements. In urging their adoption, Henry is credited with saying, "Caesar had his Brutus—Charles the first, his Cromwell—George the third—may profit by their example . . . If *this* be treason, make the most of it."

W

WESTON, Thomas (1575?–1644?). Weston helped to finance and promote the voyage of the *Mayflower* in 1620. A London ironmonger, he joined a group of English merchants interested in starting a colony in America for commercial purposes. Weston obtained a patent from the Virginia Company and organized an expedition of prospective immigrants. They included adventurers, settlers, and about 35 Separatists from the Church of England who were living in Holland. However, a dispute arose over the terms of the venture, and some members doubted whether the Virginia Company's patent was legal. Weston backed out of the enterprise, and the *Mayflower* sailed without him to Plymouth. Weston then helped to outfit and dispatch to Plymouth a second vessel, the *Fortune,* in 1621. He himself set out for the colony in 1622 with a ragtag collection of fortune hunters. Although shipwrecked and stripped of his possessions by Indians, Weston finally arrived at Plymouth. However, he was not welcomed, chiefly because he continually sought loans and was considered a troublemaker. In 1624, he went to Virginia, where he gained membership in the **House of Burgesses** (*see*) four years later. He subsequently moved to Maryland, received a grant of 1,200 acres in 1642, and became a member of the Maryland Assembly. Weston returned to England, where he died in Bristol.

WHIPPLE, Abraham (1733–1819). Whipple was a leader of the Rhode Island colonists (*see pp. 164–165*) who burned the British customs schooner **Gaspee** (*see*) on June 10, 1772. Born in Providence in 1733, he became a sailor early in life and was involved in the West India trade. Whipple was appointed commodore of the small Rhode Island fleet in 1775 and became the first American to capture a British vessel. He was soon made a commodore in the Continental Navy. In 1779, he commanded a fleet that captured eight British merchant ships carrying cargoes valued at more than $1,000,000. Later the same year, Whipple was taken prisoner by the British while defending Charleston, South Carolina. After the war, he traveled to Ohio and became a farmer. He was granted a pension by Congress in 1811 and died on May 27, 1819.

WHITE, John (1590–1645). Although he never went to America himself, White, a minister from Dorchester, England, helped Puritans find a refuge in New England. In 1624, he and other shareholders of the Dorchester Company sponsored an expedition of about 50 men to establish a fishing and farming community at Cape Ann, near the present site of Gloucester, Massachusetts. The settlers were supposed to spread the word of God as well as provide profits for the company. However, the venture failed. Those who did not return to England moved on to

Puritan tombstones often revealed an obsession with life after death.

Naumkeag (Salem) in 1626. Two years later, White helped to form the New England Company, which obtained a patent to colonize the regions between the Charles and Merrimac Rivers in Massachusetts. Led by **John Endecott** (*see*), 40 members of the company migrated to Salem. Through White's efforts, the Puritans procured in 1629 a charter from **Charles II** (*see*) that absorbed the New England Company into the **Massachusetts Bay Company** (*see*).

WIGGLESWORTH, Michael (1631–1705). A Puritan clergyman, Wigglesworth wrote a poem about the evils of immorality that became an immediate best seller and remained the most popular American poem until the 19th century. Wigglesworth, a native of Yorkshire, England, migrated to the Massachusetts Bay Colony in 1638. He graduated from Harvard College in 1651, and three years later he became minister of the Congregational Church at Malden, where he officiated for the rest of his life. His 896-line poem, *The Day of Doom, A Poetical Description of the Great and Last Judgment,* was published in 1662. It is deeply pious in tone and describes the horrible punishments awaiting anyone who dies without repenting the sins of adul-

tery, cursing, drinking, irreligious statements, and witchcraft. The poem was widely read in Puritan New England. Some historians believe that the fear it aroused may have contributed to the mass hysteria that reached a peak during the **Salem witchcraft trials** (*see*) of 1692.

WILLIAMS, Roger (1603–1683). Williams, the founder of Rhode Island, was the leading spokesman for religious freedom in the early New England colonies. Although ordained an Anglican minister in England in 1629, he set sail the following year for New England in the hope of finding a place where freedom of worship was allowed. Williams quickly discovered that the Puritan religion in the Massachusetts Bay Colony was as restrictive as the Church of England had been in England. After refusing a ministry at the Church of Boston, he preached for a short time in Plymouth and then accepted a pastorate at Salem in 1634. There Williams accused the Massachusetts magistrates of taking over lands rightfully belonging to the Indians. He also denounced the connection between the colony's government and the Puritan Church. As a result, Williams was tried for heresy in 1635 and found

Roger Williams

guilty. He and his followers were expelled from Massachusetts. They went to Rhode Island, where they were befriended by the Narraganset Indians, from whom they purchased land in 1636. Williams named the settlement Providence, "in a Sence of God's mercefull providence unto me." Its government became America's first experiment in democracy. All family heads could vote, the ownership of land was opened to all settlers, and there was a rigid separation between church and state. Williams established a Baptist church at Providence in 1639, but shortly afterward he became a so-called Seeker without any church affiliation. After traveling to England twice to get charters for Providence and other newly established communities in Rhode Island, Williams served as president of the colony (1654–1657). He saw to it that anyone was permitted to settle in Rhode Island no matter

what his rank, race, or religion was. Jews and many **Quakers** (*see*) who had been persecuted and banished by Massachusetts authorities settled in the colony. Despite Williams' support of Indian rights, the Narragansets joined other New England tribes in **King Philip's War** (*see*) in the mid-1670s, and Williams fought against them. Afterward, he served in town affairs until his death in the winter of 1683.

WINSLOW, Edward (1595–1655). A shrewd businessman and able diplomat, Winslow devoted much of his career to handling the political affairs of the Plymouth Colony in America and England. Winslow arrived at Plymouth aboard the *Mayflower* in 1620, and the next year he was chosen the Pilgrims' envoy to meet Chief Massasoit (?–1661) of the Wampanoag tribe. Winslow negotiated a treaty with the chief in 1621 and later helped to save Massasoit's life when the chief was very ill. In 1623, the colony sent Winslow to England to secure funds and provisions. He returned the following year with "3. heifers and a bull, the first beginning of any catle of that kind in ye land." Winslow subsequently served on the governor's council (1624–1646) and was elected governor three times. He is credited with contributing more than any other Pilgrim to the commercial success of Plymouth by exploring New England and establishing trading posts at Cape Ann and Buzzard's Bay and in Connecticut and Maine. He returned to England in 1646, and in 1654 was appointed a commissioner by **Oliver Cromwell** (*see*) on an expedition against the Spanish West Indies. The fleet captured Jamaica. Winslow died of fever on the return voyage on May 8, 1655.

He is the only Pilgrim of whom a portrait is known to exist. His son Josiah (1629?–1680) became governor of Plymouth Colony in 1673, the first native-born American to hold that office.

WINTHROP, John (1588–1649). The first governor of the Massachusetts Bay Colony, Winthrop guided the Puritans through their first difficult years in America. In 1629, worried about his declining law practice in London and the future of Puritanism in England, Winthrop joined the **Massachusetts Bay Company** (*see*), which received permission from **Charles I** (*see*) to establish a self-governing community in New England. Chosen to lead a fleet carrying about 700 colonists, Winthrop sailed on the *Arbella* (*see*) in 1630 and anchored at Salem, a village founded by **John Endecott** (*see*). The ranks of the settlers were soon swelled by about 1,300 new arrivals. Winthrop first decided to start a settlement at Charlestown but changed his mind and selected a site, later named Boston, to be the capital of the colony. He was elected governor 13 times and in between terms acted as deputy governor. Like other Puritan fathers, Winthrop would not tolerate dissent. Most citizens of the Massachusetts Bay Colony, including former governor **Sir Henry Vane** (*see*), opposed Winthrop's banishment of **Anne Hutchinson** (*see*) for her religious views in 1637. Although the prevailing trend in the colony was toward democracy, Winthrop defended the need for an absolute ruler. In an article written in 1642, he tried to show that there was no precedent for democracy in England or in the Old Testament. Two years later, he wrote an even stronger condemnation of democratic government. This caused much public protest, and Winthrop was severely criticized. Winthrop's views on democracy became somewhat more favorable by 1645, when he made a speech defining liberty as meaning freedom within the limits of the law. The speech restored Winthrop's popularity, and he was elected governor every year until his death in 1649.

WOLFE, James (1727–1759). One of England's most outstanding young officers, Wolfe was only 31 years old when he was promoted to major general and assigned to launch an assault on Quebec during the **French and Indian War** (*see*). Wolfe had already served with distinction under **Jeffrey Amherst** (*see*) at the siege of Fort Louisbourg in 1758. In June of the following year, Wolfe landed with a 9,000-man force on the south shore of the St. Lawrence River, opposite Quebec, and began shelling the city. Wolfe's first attempt to capture it on July 31 was repulsed. However, in a second attack, which was launched on September 13, the British successfully engaged the French on the Plains of Abraham. The French, commanded by the **Marquis Louis Joseph de Montcalm** (*see*), were forced to surrender. Both commanders were fatally wounded in the battle (*see pp. 118–121*). Wolfe died shortly after his army's victory was assured. With the capture of Quebec, all of French Canada soon fell into British hands.

Z

ZENGER, John Peter (1697–1746). This German-born printer was the defendant in a trial that established the principle of freedom of the press in the American colonies. At issue was whether colonial authorities had the right to censor opponents. Zenger, who had emigrated in 1710, started the *New York Weekly Journal* in 1733. He was backed by wealthy merchants who opposed the policies of the colonial governor, William Cosby (1690?–1736?). The *Journal* consistently printed attacks on Cosby. On November 17, 1734, he had Zenger arrested for libel. Zenger was kept in jail until the start of his trial on August 4, 1735. However, he continued to edit the *Journal* by giving instructions to his wife through a hole in the prison door. The judge at Zenger's trial, following the rules of English law, refused to allow testimony that might prove Zenger's accusations. Instead, he instructed the jury to decide if the statements in question had actually been printed. The judge, a supporter of Cosby, would then determine if the statements were libelous. Andrew Hamilton (?–1741), Zenger's lawyer, eloquently persuaded the jury to ignore the judge's ruling and to decide the case on its own. Zenger was acquitted. This was the first time that a case of libel had been decided by a jury. The practice later became standard procedure in libel cases and freed the press from censorship by biased judges. Zenger subsequently published a complete account of his trial. As a reward for his services, he was made public printer of the New York Colony in 1737 and was appointed to the same post in New Jersey the following year. After Zenger's death on July 28, 1746, his widow and then his son John continued the publication of the *Journal* until 1751.

In one of his first issues, Zenger attacked British officials in 1733.